ROMANTIC CROCHET

30 Beautiful Projects for your Home

RHODA ROBERTSON

Trafalgar Square Publishing

ACKNOWLEDGEMENTS

For me, this book on crochet lace is a dream come true, a chance to pass on my ideas to like-minded people. My most grateful thanks to Ena McKeeman for checking all my patterns and diagrams so thoroughly and with such accuracy, to Vivien Oliver, my sister, whose nimble fingers hammered endlessly at the computer, converting my notes into legible text, to Julie Matthews for her constructive ideas and clever ways with words and to all the other ladies who gave their time and help so generously. I am much indebted to my crochet students for testing the patterns and producing some of the crochet items included in this book, especially Moira Dow, Daphne Fretwell, Catherine Aitken, Jan Heriot and Jennifer Thomson. A special thanks to my friends, Sylvia Cosh and James Walters for their help and guidance, to Munni Srivastava of Savitri Books, the sole orchestrator of this book, whose good planning at every stage made it all possible. Cheerful Odile Noël, 'translator extraordinaire', I thank you too. My gratitude also to my family and friends for their encouragement and good humour over the many months of hard work. Finally, a huge thank you to my husband Stuart for his patience, understanding and support during my time-out from other 'pleasures' (such as housework) and for giving me confidence throughout.

Rhoda Robertson, Edinburgh, July 1998.

First published in the United States of America in 1999 by
TRAFALGAR SQUARE PUBLISHING
North Pomfret, Vermont 05053

Printed and bound in Spain

Library of Congress Catalog Card Number – 98-84036

ISBN 1-57076-119-1

Original English edition
published by
SAVITRI BOOKS LIMITED
115J Cleveland Street
London W1P 5PN

Art direction and design by Mrinalini Srivastava
Photography by Sarah Dewe

Typeset in 11/14 Sabon
Reproduced by Regent Publishing Services, Hong Kong
Printed and bound by Gráficas Reunidas, Spain

IMPORTANT NOTICES

The author and publishers advise the readers of this book to photocopy the diagrams which accompany each project. These can be enlarged to facilitate the reading of the symbols and each row colored as the work proceeds. However, the author and publishers advise readers to take careful note of the photocopying and copyright reproduction laws that apply to other sources of designs. The projects contained in this book are all original designs and are the property of the author. Anyone wanting to use these designs, wholly or partly, for commercial purposes, should seek permission from the copyright owners.

The author and publishers of this book have made every effort to ensure that the instructions contained in the book are accurate and complete. They cannot, however, be responsible for human error, typographical mistakes, or variations in individual work.

CONTENTS

INTRODUCTION

Ever since I was around fifteen years old and sat spellbound as my aunt was teaching me how to crochet, I have been fascinated by the diversity of patterns and textures which can be created with a few simple stitches. Since then, I am seldom without my hooks and yarns and I find it difficult to resist the temptation to pick up my hook and work just another few rows...

Over the years I have experimented with texture, color and pattern and much of my work has been exhibited. I have always had a strong commitment to promote textile crafts and I was fortunate to have the opportunity to do so through craft guilds, exhibitions, displays and workshops across my native Scotland. One of my greatest joys is to pass on my knowledge and experience to others in the workshops and courses I teach. It is always exciting to meet other enthusiasts who share my passion for crochet. Their eagerness to learn has been an encouragement and an inspiration. For several years, I have had the privilege of judging for the Handcraft Section of the Royal Highland Show in Edinburgh, a prestigious open competition which attracts entries of a very high standard, world-wide.

The collection of lace crochet projects contained in this book represents some of my recent work, but also includes some of my students' favorites. There is, I hope, something to please everyone, with projects ranging in size and complexity and using a variety of lace techniques. The romantic charm of this versatile craft has been adapted to suit contemporary taste and you will experience the thrill of creating small personal treasures, attractive gifts for someone special or items for your own home – tomorrow's family heirlooms.

A BRIEF HISTORY OF CROCHET

Very little is known of the origins of crochet; some say it originated in Biblical times, maybe as long ago as 950 BC, during the days of Solomon. Fragments of crochet work have been found in Egypt and in ancient Babylon which was a wool trade center. The Babylonians were fond of elaborate woollen clothes and it is more than likely that these were knitted or crocheted. Ancient crochet patterns found in the Middle East and North Africa suggest that crochet has been around for thousands of years.

'Shepherd's knitting' is a delightful term which was used long ago in Scotland. Sheep's wool caught on fencing and bushes was gathered by the shepherds and, after spinning into a rough wool, it would be made into simple garments, using a stick with a crude hook carved at one end. Crochet has come a long way since then!

The rapid mechanization of the weaving process affected some of the traditional methods of producing fabrics such as crochet and knitting, which suffered badly and almost died out. For a long time crochet was made by nuns and was confined behind the walls of convents. In early 19th-century Britain, however, lace trimmings were becoming fashionable and crochet was revived as a suitable accomplishment for well-to-do young ladies. The new mills now spun fine cotton yarn which offered new possibilities for the exponents of the craft. Around the same time, crochet in Ireland became an important cottage industry and ever since, Irish crochet has really been a craft in its own right.

The Victorian period witnessed the ever-growing popularity of crochet. Contemporary paintings and photographs of Victorian interiors show how every available surface – furniture, shelves, the piano even – was covered with doilies, antimacassars and flounces made of crochet lace. The enthusiasm for the craft generated an enormous wealth of designs and intricate patterns. If you have a textile museum near you, it is well worth a visit, as the wonderful work of days gone by can be a great source of inspiration to the modern maker. The tablecloth on the frontispiece of this book was made at the turn of the century and inspired the pattern of the one shown on page 95.

BEFORE YOU START

At the beginning of each project you will find one of the following symbols:

They indicate the degree of complexity of the particular project. One crochet hook indicates a good starting project, two hooks are for the fairly experienced worker and three accompany projects which represent more of a challenge. Although this book is not primarily designed for the complete newcomer to the craft, all the projects are fully explained and are sufficiently varied to appeal to a wide range of ability. Choose your first project carefully and you will soon gain the experience and the confidence required to tackle the more complex designs.

WORKING NOTES

◆ Tension / Gauge

It is important to make a sample before you embark on your chosen project, as it is the only way to check whether the tension / gauge (the number of stitches and/or spaces over a given measurement) is correct. An incorrect or uneven tension means that the finished piece of work will be smaller or larger than the desired size or that the work will not lie flat. If the sample is smaller and tighter than it should be, try using a larger hook; if it is bigger or looser, use a smaller hook. When a pattern does not specify a tension check, refer to the finished size of the object to guide

you. Beginners often have problems with uneven tension. This will be corrected by practice.

◆ Quantities of crochet thread

Most of the projects in this book were worked using bedspread-weight cotton thread / No 10 and a No 7 / 1.50 mm crochet hook. Some can also be made using a finer cotton thread / No 20 with a N0 8 / 1.25 mm crochet hook, which produce a smaller version of the project. The amounts given are sufficient to allow for slight differences in tension or size of hook which may influence the quantity of thread required. Some of the smaller items use such a small amount of thread that it is difficult to specify accurately. You may be able to make several items from one small ball. If you substitute a different brand of cotton, you should note that 'bedspread-weight cotton thread' can vary in weight and texture from one manufacturer to another. Check your tension carefully and make sure you have sufficient yarn to complete the pattern, as two batches of cotton may vary considerably in color.

◆ DIAGRAMS

All the projects in this book are accompanied by one or several diagrams. These are based on symbols which represent the various stitches (see the list of abbreviations and symbols and crochet terms on page 10). Familiarize yourself with them if you are a beginner. They provide a visual way of checking the number of stitches at a glance. Even if you are not used to working from diagrams, do give them a try as they are an invaluable aid to checking the accuracy of your work. It is important to read through to the end of the pattern before you begin and to refer to the diagram as you work. As you tackle each row or round, always read to the end of the instruction before you start, as the beginning and the finish are usually different from the middle section. Make a photocopy of the diagrams, enlarging them if necessary, as it has not always been possible to fit all the written instructions next to the relevant diagram. Color each row or round as you work to keep track of where you are.

ABBREVIATIONS & SYMBOLS

This is a list of abbreviated crochet terms as used in the written instructions for the projects included in this book. The symbols identify the various stitches used within the diagrams. **This glossary is not exhaustive but includes solely the stitches actually used in this book.**

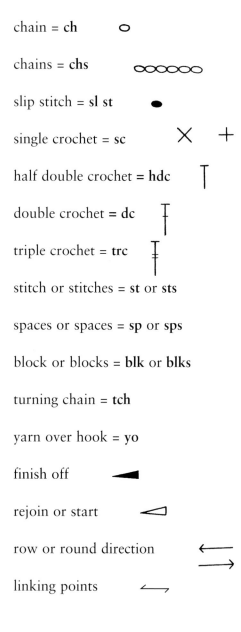

chain = **ch**

chains = **chs**

slip stitch = **sl st**

single crochet = **sc**

half double crochet = **hdc**

double crochet = **dc**

triple crochet = **trc**

stitch or stitches = **st** or **sts**

spaces or spaces = **sp** or **sps**

block or blocks = **blk** or **blks**

turning chain = **tch**

yarn over hook = **yo**

finish off

rejoin or start

row or round direction

linking points

POINTS TO REMEMBER

- ◆ Asterisks * in a series of instructions denote a part of the pattern to be repeated.
- ◆ Brackets ( ) represent a series of stitches to be worked into a stitch, space or loop, a specified number of times.
- ◆ The diagrams in this book always show the right side of the work.
- ◆ The numbers written in **bold** characters at the center of the circular diagrams denote the number of starting chains. The other figures denote the **row** or **round** number, or the number of ch sts within a pattern, e.g. loops or spaces.
- ◆ The loop on the hook is referred to as the **working loop** and is never counted as a chain stitch. After completing a stitch or group of stitches, there should be only one loop on the hook – **the working loop.**
- ◆ Always insert the hook under the top two threads of the stitch, unless otherwise stated.
- ◆ **Right side – wrong side.** Due to the way in which the thread is twisted during the work, slight differences appear in the upper and the underside of the piece. When several pieces of work must be joined, great care must be taken not to confuse the two sides. Marking the wrong side with a contrasting thread is good practice.
- ◆ Thread quantities and hook sizes are specified in Imperial and metric throughout the book.

CROCHET STITCHES USED IN THIS BOOK

All crochet begins with a slip loop or a knot, followed by the required number of chain stitches. To make a slip loop, fold a short length of yarn to make a loop, insert hook into this loop and catch the long end of the thread, draw through (diagram 1) and tighten, till the loop slides easily along the hook (diagram 2). The slip loop is not a stitch but is referred to as the working loop.

DIAGRAM 1   DIAGRAM 2

Chain stitch (ch st). Yarn over hook (yo) and draw it through the loop on the hook – one ch st is made (diagram 1). Continue till required number of ch sts are made (diagram 2). This is called the starting or foundation chain.

DIAGRAM 1   DIAGRAM 2

Slip stitch (sl st). Work a short chain. Insert hook in the second ch from the hook under the top two threads of ch st (diagram 1), yo and draw yarn through ch st and the remaining loop on the hook (diagram 2). One sl st is made.

DIAGRAM 1   DIAGRAM 2

Single crochet (sc) Work a short ch. Always make sure you are working into the front / right side of the ch. Insert hook in second ch from hook, under the top two threads of ch st, leaving a single thread underneath the hook (diagram 1).

DIAGRAM 1

Yo and draw yarn back through ch st, 2 loops on the hook. Yo and draw through the remaining 2 loops on hook (diagram 2). One sc is made (diagram 3).

DIAGRAM 2   DIAGRAM 3

Half double crochet (hdc). Yo, insert hook in third ch from hook (diagram 1), yo and draw yarn back through ch st, pulling yarn up slightly, 3 loops on hook. Yo and draw through all 3 loops on hook (diagram 2). One hdc is made (diagram 3).

DIAGRAM 1   DIAGRAM 2

DIAGRAM 3

Double crochet (dc)

Yo, insert hook in fourth ch from hook (diagram 1), yo and draw yarn back through ch st, pulling yarn up slightly, 3 loops on hook (diagram 2). Yo and draw through two loops only, yo again and draw through remaining two loops (diagram 3). One dc is made (diagram 4).

DIAGRAM 1   DIAGRAM 2

DIAGRAM 3   DIAGRAM 4

11

Triple crochet (trc). Yo twice, insert hook in 5th chain from hook (diagram 1), yo and draw back through ch st, pulling yarn up slightly, 4 loops on hook. *yo and draw through 2 loops only (diagram 2). Repeat from* 2 more times (diagram 3 and 4), till one loop remains. One trc made (diagram 5).

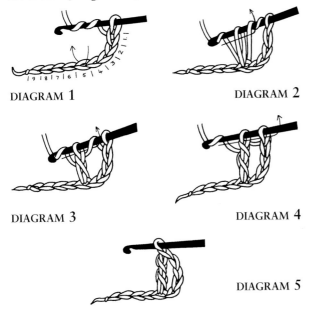

DIAGRAM 1

DIAGRAM 2

DIAGRAM 3

DIAGRAM 4

DIAGRAM 5

FILET CROCHET

Filet crochet is the name given to regular open network (or mesh) worked in fine cotton using dc and chs. The designs are produced by 'filling in' some of the spaces with double crochet, called blocks (blks) and leaving other spaces open to create the pattern. Maintaining a firm and even tension throughout is very important. The blocks should be fairly solid to show the design to the best effect. Change hook size till you get the correct tension. In the patterns which accompany the projects in this book, the blks are represented by the symbol ✕ the sps are left blank.

There are two ways of producing the mesh, each creating a slightly different effect. These differ in the number of chs used to produce the mesh or open sps and the number of dc used to form the blks. The particular method used is specified with each pattern. Make sure you use the correct one.

Method 1 (probably the most commonly used) consists of ch2 sps between 4dc blks. The finished work will be square with a fairly open texture.

Method 2 consists of ch1 sp between 3dc blks. The spaces in the mesh are rectangular and the finished work has a closer texture (diagram 2).

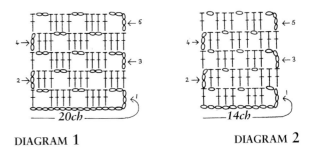

DIAGRAM 1

DIAGRAM 2

WORKING IN THE ROUND (using the sl st)

The same basic stitches are used when working in a circle, but the starting ch is joined by a slip stitch (sl st) to form a ring. Once the ring is formed, the motif or circular pattern is worked from the center outward, increasing the number of stitches on each round to keep the work flat. At the start of each new round ch sts are worked to equal the height of the stitches being used on the next round. These are the equivalent of 'turning chains' and may be counted as a stitch.

To form a ring, work the required number of ch sts, insert hook in the first ch st made, yo and draw through ch st **and** the remaining loop on the hook (diagram 1). One sl st is made and the starting ring is formed (diagram 2). At the start of the first round, work the required number of ch sts to equal the height of sts on the first round. Work the stitches into the ring, **not** into the ch sts (diagram 3). To complete the first round, work a sl st into the top of the turning chain at the beginning of the round (diagram 4).

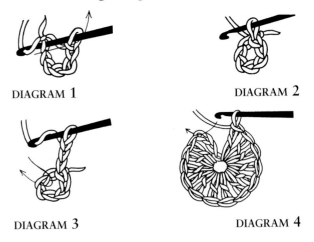

DIAGRAM 1

DIAGRAM 2

DIAGRAM 3

DIAGRAM 4

STITCHES FOR SPECIAL EFFECTS

ch3 picot
Work ch3, sl st into the 3rd ch from hook, pull tight.

ch4 picot
Work ch4, sl st into 4th ch from hook, pull tight.

ch5 picot
Work ch5, sl st into 5th ch from hook, pull tight.

5 loop puff st
It is worked using extended hdc as follows: *yo, insert hook into st, catch thread, draw through a long loop, up to ¼ in, 3 loops on hook, Repeat from* 4 more times in the same stitch. Finally, catch the thread and draw firmly through all 11 loops. A tight ch st may be added after the puff st to secure.

Single crochet (sc) variation
Work as a basic sc, but insert the hook in the back single thread only to create a ridged effect.

Double crochet (dc) variation
Work as a basic dc, but insert the hook in the back single thread only to create a ridged effect. This technique can also be used with hdc and trc. The ridges will appear on the right side of the work.

TO INCREASE

Increase 2sc
2 complete sc together in 1 stitch.

Increase 3sc
3 complete sc together in 1 stitch.

Increase 2hdc
2 complete hdc together in 1 stitch.

Increase 3hdc
3 complete hdc together in 1 stitch.

Increase 2dc
2 complete dc together in 1 stitch.

Increase 3dc
3 complete dc together in 1 stitch.

Increase 2trc
2 complete trc together in 1 stitch.

Increase 3trc
3 complete trc together in 1 stitch.

TO DECREASE

Decrease 2sc
hook in the first st, catch thread, draw loop through, hook in next st, catch thread, draw loop through, catch thread again and draw through all 3 loops on hook.

Decrease 3sc
as above, but work over 3 separate sts, finally taking the thread through all 4 loops on the hook.

Decrease 2hdc
1hdc worked to first stage (3 loops on hook), 1hdc in next st to first stage (5 loops on hook), catch thread, draw through all 5 loops on hook.

Decrease 3hdc
as above, but work over 3 separate sts, taking thread through all 7 loops on hook.

Decrease 2dc
1dc worked to last stage but one (2 loops on hook), 1dc in next to last stage but one (3 loops on hook), catch thread and draw through all 3 loops on hook.

Decrease 3dc
as above, but work over 3 separate sts, taking thread through all 4 loops on hook.

Decrease 2trc
1trc worked to last stage but one (2 loops on hook) 1trc in next st to last stage but one (3 loops on hook), catch thread and draw through all 3 loops on hook.

Decrease 3trc
as above, but work over 3 separate sts, finally taking thread through all 4 loops on hook.

WORKING NOTES

- To **finish off** and secure the last stitch, cut the thread at approximately 6 in from the **working loop,** draw tail end through loop and pull gently till tight.
- Always leave a good length of thread when you make the slip loop at the start of the foundation chain. If you reach the end of the first row to discover that you are short

of chain stitches, simply remove the hook from the loop and insert it into the first ch, pull the thread through and add the required number of chs, plus one extra. Pull the tail end through the last ch loop to finish off. Now continue the pattern.

- **Turning chains** are used to move on to the next row or round. The number of turning chains used is usually equivalent to the height of the first stitch at the start of the next row or round, 1 or 2ch for a single crochet; 2ch for a half double crochet; 3ch for a double crochet. In some cases, especially with longer stitches, the turning chain is counted as a stitch. This is specified in the instructions for each project.

- **Problems with the starting chain**. If you have too many chs at the end of the first row, disregard them and carefully unpick them when the project is complete or weave them into the back of the work. If the starting chain always turns out to be too tight and difficult to work into, try using a larger hook to make the starting chain, returning to the original hook size for the remainder of the pattern. Similarly, work the starting chain with a smaller hook, if it tends to be loose

- **Joining yarns.** A join should be almost invisible and not create an unsightly lump in the work. This is even more important with crochet lace. If possible, make the join close to a solid part of the design or near the edge, rather than in the middle of an open mesh section.

There are two ways of joining thread of the same color:

1. Before finishing the ball of cotton, while there are still some 6 in left, take the beginning of the new ball, tie the two tail ends together and tighten the knot. Pull the tails through to the wrong side of the work and weave in both ends separately.

2. Insert the hook into the next stitch, pull the loop through from the old ball and finish the stitch by dropping the thread from the old ball. Catch the tail end from the new ball to complete the stitch, pull both tails firmly to the wrong side of the work and weave in each thread separately, in different directions.

ADVICE TO LEFT-HANDERS

As most crocheters are right-handed, the diagrams have been drawn to suit them. If you are left-handed, there are ways of transferring the diagrams. The traditional method is to stand the book up and hold a square mirror at right angles to the page. This is a little awkward, but it will give you a reversed image to work from. A far better solution is to use a photocopier to print the design on tracing paper. Turn the paper over to follow the reversed working diagram, any figures appearing on the diagram can then be viewed from the right side of the copy. The written instructions remain the same.

AFTERCARE OF CROCHET LACE

All the projects in this book are made in pure cotton thread which is a very resistant material. A gentle hand wash is recommended, using pure soap flakes or a mild liquid detergent. Rinse well. Do not wring. Absorb the excess water by spreading the item over a large towel, roll up carefully and press gently down with your hands. A slight shrinkage may occur but, while the lace is still damp, it is possible to ease the work back to its original size by pulling it gently and evenly by hand or by pinning it out and allowing it to dry in position. This process is known as blocking.

Stubborn stains on white cotton items, can usually be removed by steeping the piece for twenty minutes in a bleach solution (use 1 tablespoonful of bleach to 2 pints of tepid water).

BLOCKING & IRONING

If the work does not require washing, it should be steam-pressed lightly on the wrong side, using a damp cloth. Washed pieces should be left on a thick towel, till almost dry. Cover a large piece of cardboard with plastic wrap. Draw a template of the outer shape of the article on a piece of plain paper (tinted paper is even better under a piece made of white cotton thread). Use a compass for circular pieces. Graph paper is ideal for square or oblong designs. Slip this template under the plastic wrap and pin in place at the corners. Right side facing, ease the work till it fits the drawn shape, then pin out using stainless steel pins. Do not overstretch the work. Once the main shape is set in place, open out the picots, pull out all points gently, ease the loops and curves, making sure they match all round. Use as many pins as necessary. If the work begins to dry out before the pinning is finished, dampen it lightly using a water spray. Leave to dry completely before removing the pins. With filet crochet, make sure that all the blocks and spaces are square and well aligned, and that all edges are straight. The blocking process should be repeated each time the article is washed.

Crochet work can benefit from a light starching. Spray starch available in cans gives very good results and is easier to use than conventional starch.

SEWING PATTERNS FOR THE TISSUE BOX LINING AND THE VANITY POUCH
(See pages 85 and 58, respectively.)

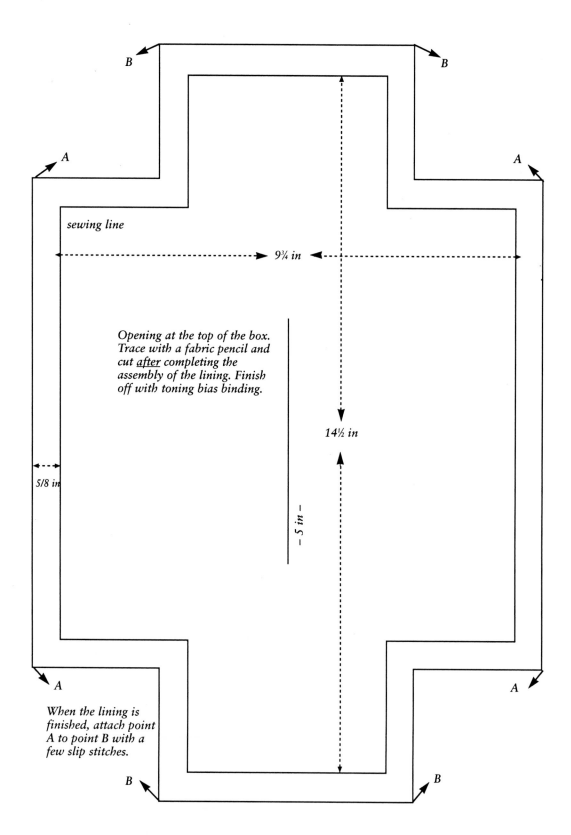

B

B

A

A

sewing line

9¾ in

*Opening at the top of the box.
Trace with a fabric pencil and
cut after completing the
assembly of the lining. Finish
off with toning bias binding.*

14½ in

– 5 in –

5/8 in

A

A

*When the lining is
finished, attach point
A to point B with a
few slip stitches.*

B

B

OPPOSITE: PATTERN FOR THE TISSUE BOX LINING (see page 85)
Enlarge this pattern by 200%. Cut twice. Right sides together, pin the two layers together. Machine-stitch, leaving a 2 in gap for turning the work. Trim off excess cloth. Clip the seam in the angles down to the sewing line. Press. Slip stitch the gap. Cut out the top opening and neaten the edges with bias binding.

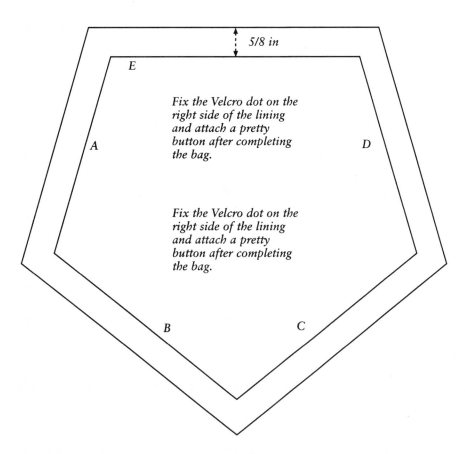

ABOVE: PATTERN FOR THE VANITY POUCH (see page 58)
Enlarge this pattern by 200%. Cut twice out of the top fabric and twice out of the lining material. Right sides together, pin the two sides of the pouch. Machine-stitch along the sewing lines from A to D. Repeat for the lining. Cut off the excess fabric. Clip the angles down to the sewing line. Turn out the pouch and its lining. Press. Fold the top of the bag along the sewing line. Repeat for the lining. Press. Insert the lining inside the pouch. Pin and slip-stich the lining to the top of the bag. Press. Fix the Velcro dot to the lining. Attach the lace panel to the front of the pouch and add a pretty button.

Overleaf. The red cushion is produced by using nine of the motifs which are used to form the place mat.

PLACE MATS & MATCHING COASTERS

Each place mat is made up of six identical motifs, joined together and framed by a large border. The coaster consists of a single motif, with a narrow edge. One such motif could also be appliqued in the corner of a napkin. Nine of these squares were worked in bright red cotton and were used to form the top of the cushion, shown opposite. This panel was appliqued over a cover made of bright red toning silk and finished off with small tassels. Make up a cushion or applique the panel over a ready-made cover.

Approximate sizes: Coaster – 1 motif, including edging: 5 in square. Place mat – 6 motifs, including edging: 16½ x 12½ in. Cushion – 9 motifs: 15 x 15 in

MATERIALS. Place mat and coaster: 3 oz / 75 g white bedspread-weight cotton thread / No 10. Cushion: 4 oz / 100 g, red bedspread-weight cotton thread / No 10, a No 7 / 1.50 mm crochet hook, an 18 in cushion pad

WORKING NOTES
- Always check number of ch sts on every round, especially from round 7 (see diagram 1, page 20).
- Rounds 7, 8, 9 and 10. Please note the second sl st at the ends of these rounds, before the start of the next round.
- On round 9, the sc is worked over and around, incorporating the ch sts from the previous 2 rounds.
- Refer to the stitch diagram as you work, making a photocopy is helpful.

TO MAKE ONE MOTIF
(excluding edge): ch6, sl st to form a ring (see diagram 1, **first motif**).

Round 1   ch2 (to count as 1sc), 7sc in ring (8sc altogether), sl st to ch-2 to complete round.

Round 2   ch7, 1dc in next sc, *ch4, 1dc in next sc, repeat from* 5 more times. End with ch4, sl st to 3rd of ch-7 at the beginning of the round(8sps).

Round 3   ch3 (to count as 1dc), 2dc at the base of ch3, *ch4, skip 4ch, 3dc together in the next dc, repeat from* till the end of the round. End with ch4, sl st to the 3rd of ch-3.

Round 4   ch3 (to count as 1dc), 2dc in next dc, 1dc in next dc, *ch4, skip 4ch, 1dc in dc, 2dc together in next dc, 1dc in next dc, repeat from* till the end of the round. End with ch4, a sl st to the 3rd of ch-3 at the beginning of the round.

Rounds 5 to 11   Continue to work as per diagram 1. Finish off, weave in ends.

LINKING MOTIFS. These are joined by crocheting together as you complete the last full round. Join motifs in the order and position shown in diagram 1. The symbol ⟵⟶ denotes the linking points.

TO MAKE A PLACE MAT (6 motifs). Begin by making one complete motif as above. Work a second motif, but leave the last full edge unworked and, while working on it, link motifs together using a sl st at the points shown on the

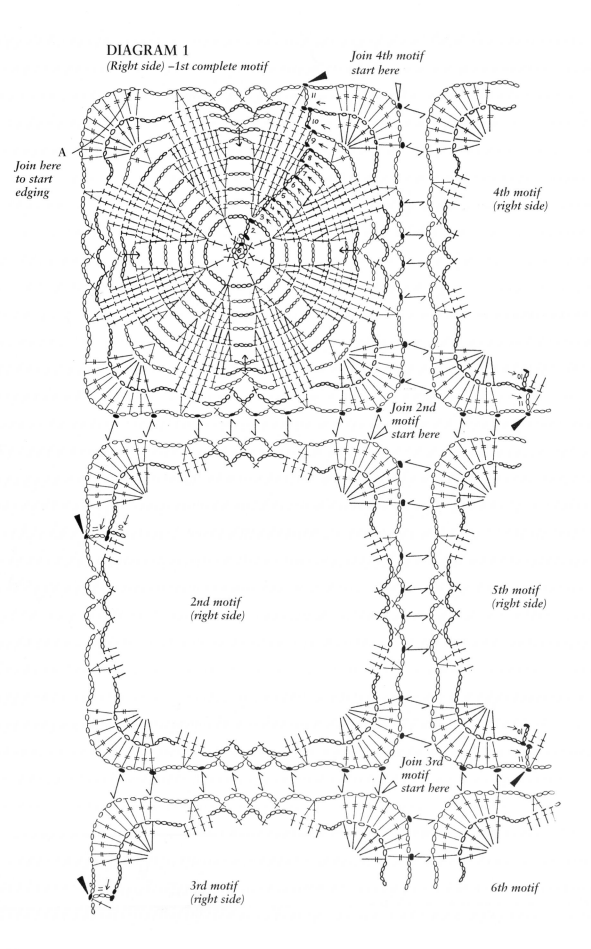

DIAGRAM 1
(Right side) −1st complete motif

Join 4th motif
start here

A

*Join here
to start
edging*

4th motif
(right side)

Join 2nd
motif
start here

2nd motif
(right side)

5th motif
(right side)

Join 3rd
motif
start here

3rd motif
(right side)

6th motif

diagram. Work to 7th trc on the second last corner group of sts, sl st across to the **first motif** (pushing the hook through the wrong side under the top 2 threads of trc opposite). Complete the corner group of sts and, after the last trc, work a sl st across to last trc as before. Continue to complete the **second motif** and, at the same time, link across to the first motif, as shown on the diagram. Do not rush the process of linking the motifs. Finish off.

Third motif – Join in the same way as second motif, starting at the point shown on diagram.

Fourth motif – Join to the right hand side of the first motif.

Fifth motif – Leave 2 full edges unworked and link as before to the fourth and second motifs.

Sixth motif – Work as fifth motif, but linking to the fifth and third motifs.

This completes the main section of the place mat.

EDGING FOR THE PLACE MAT

WORKING NOTES
◆ Before beginning the edge, **mark the center ch-1 sp** at each of the 4 corners with a safety pin, for future reference. Remove and replace as required.
◆ Refer to the diagram on page 23 and work all chs and sc firmly.

BEGIN. Join the thread to point **A,** in first ch-1 space of the corner group (see diagram 2, opposite).

Round 1   ch3 to count as first dc, 1dc in same sp, 2dc in each next 3 x ch-1 sps, 3dc in next sp (marked space), 2dc in each next 4 x ch-1 sps. This completes a corner group of 19dc. *ch5, 1sc in ch-5 loop, repeat from* 5 more times, ch5, 2dc in each next 5 x ch-1 sps (10dc), skip the seam/join. 2dc in each of 5 x ch-1 sps in the corner group of the next motif (check the diagram), *ch5, sc in ch-5 loop, repeat from* 5 more times, ch5, 2dc in each next 5 x ch-1 sps (10tr), skip seam/join, 2dc in each of 5 x ch-1 sps in the corner group of the next motif. *ch5, 1sc in the next ch-5 loop, repeat from* 5 times. ch5, 2dc in each next 4 x ch-1 sps, 3dc in the next sp (marked corner space), 2dc in each next 4 x ch-1 sps. Continue to work the remaining 3 sides, following the diagram and **remembering** to work 3dc together in the center of the marked sp at each corner. End with a sl st to the 3rd of ch-3 at the beginning of the round.

Mark the first of ch5 on each of the following rounds to help identify the start and the finish of each round. Remove and replace the marker as you start each round.

Round 2   *ch5, skip 2dcs, 1sc in next dc, repeat from* till 6 loops made, ch5, skip ch-5 loop, sc in next ch-5 loop, *ch5, 1sc in next ch-5 loop, repeat from* 3 more times, ch5, skip ch-5 loop, 1sc in dc, ch5, skip 2dc, sc in next dc, ch5, skip 2dc, 1sc in next dc, ch5 skip 6dc, 1sc in next dc, ch5, skip 2dc, 1sc in next dc, ch5, skip 2dc, 1sc in last dc, ch5, skip ch-5 loop, 1sc in loop, continue to work round all 4 sides as shown on the diagram. End with a sl st to first of the ch-5 at the beginning of the round, sl st in each of the next 2ch.

Round 3   *ch5, 1sc in next ch-5 loop, repeat from* on all 4 sides. End with a sl st to the first of ch-5 at the beginning of the round, sl st in each of the next 2ch.

Round 4   *ch5, 1sc in the next loop, repeat from* as on round 3.

Round 5   ch5, 1sc in the next ch-5 loop, **5dc in the next sc** (first corner), 1sc in the ch-5 loop, *ch5, 1sc in next ch-5 loop, repeat from* till 10 x ch-5 loops from corner 5dc. 5dc in ch-5 loop, 1sc in next loop, *ch5, 1sc in next loop, repeat from* till 9 x ch-5 loops, 5dc in next ch-5 loop,

1sc in next loop, work 10 more loops, **5dc in next sc** (second corner), 1sc in next loop. First side is complete. Work 10 more loops, 5dc in next loop, 1sc in next loop, work 10 more loops, **5dc in next sc** (third corner), 1sc in next loop. Second side is complete. Work 10 more loops, 5dc in next loop, 1sc in next loop, work 9 loops, 5dc in next loop, 1sc in next loop, work 10 more loops, **5dc in next sc** (fourth corner), 1sc in next loop. Third side is complete. Finish the last side by working 10 more loops, 5dc in next loop, 1sc in next loop, work a further 9 loops until you reach the first ch-5 loop at the beginning of the round, sl st to the first of ch-5 to complete the round.

Round 6 sl st in each of next 2ch, work round the corner as follows: ch5, 1sc in first dc of 5dc group, ch5, skip 1dc, 1sc in next dc, ch5, skip 1dc, 1sc in last dc, *ch5, 1sc in next loop, repeat from* 9 more times, ch5, 1sc in the 3rd of 5dc group, *ch5, 1sc in next loop, repeat

from*8 more times, ch5, 1sc in 3rd of 5dc group, 10 more loops, work round the corner as before – ch5, 1sc in first dc of 5dc group, ch5, skip 1dc, 1sc in the next dc, ch5, skip 1dc, 1sc in the last dc. Continue round the remaining sides – taking care to place the sc accurately at the corners. End with a sl st to the first of ch-5 at the beginning of the round.

Round 7 sl st in each next 2ch, *ch5, 1sc in next loop, repeat from* on all 4 sides. End with a sl st to the first of ch-5.

Round 8 As round 7. End with a sl st to first of ch-5, sl st in each next 2ch.

Round 9 ch3 (to count as a dc), 1dc, 1hdc, 1sc in first loop, ch2, *(2dc, 1hdc, 1sc, ch2) in next loop, repeat from* on all 4 sides. End with a sl st to 3rd of ch-3. Finish off, weave in ends.

DIAGRAM 2
Edging for the place mat

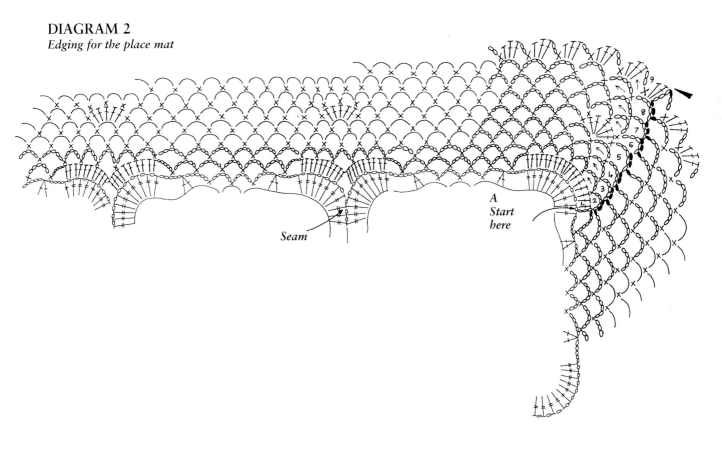

MATCHING COASTER. Make 1 complete motif. Work edgings as follows (see diagram 3, opposite). Join the thread to point **A**, in the first ch-1 sp of a corner group.

Round 1   *ch5, skip (1trc, ch1, 1trc), 1sc in next ch-1 sp, repeat from* 3 more times. *ch5, 1sc in next ch-5 loop, repeat from* 5 times. ch5, skip 1trc, 1sc in first ch-1 sp on next corner group, *ch5, skip (1trc, ch1, 1trc), 1sc in the next ch-1 sp, repeat from* 2 more times. Continue round the remaining sides following the diagram. End with a sl st to the first of ch-5.

Round 2   ch3 (to count as a dc), (1dc, 1hdc, 1sc) in first loop, ch2*(2dc, 1hdc, 1sc, ch2) in next loop, repeat from* on all 4 sides. End with a sl st to the 3rd of ch-3. Finish off, weave in ends.

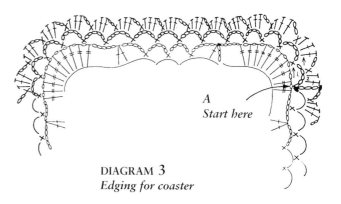

A
Start here

DIAGRAM **3**
Edging for coaster

The coaster – life-size

CUSHION PANEL BASED ON THE PLACE MAT DESIGN

Work the first 6 motifs as for the place mat. Link together. Work another 3 motifs and link to the previous ones, (see diagram 4, opposite). Weave in tail ends.

Once all the motifs are attached, press lightly on the wrong side with a damp cloth. Ease and pin into shape on a board covered with plastic wrap. Leave to dry. There is no border around the cushion. A tassel, attached to a short chain (ch12) can be added to each of the 4 corners. Attach cotton to center ch-1 sp at corners and follow the instructions for the single ch tassel, below. Slip-stitch the completed crochet panel onto the center of the cushion.

SINGLE CHAIN WITH TASSEL. Cut a length of cotton, at least 35 in. Thread through the suggested point on the pattern, under a double thread if possible, pull till the ends are of even length. In the same place, insert a slightly larger hook and work the required number of chains, using both tails together. Extend last ch loops. Remove the hook. Cut 12 short strands of cotton (8 in) and place evenly through the last ch loop. Pull loop tight. Fold strands in half and bind tightly 2 or 3 times, approximately ¼ in down from the ch loop, using the remaining cotton tails. Thread the tails through a darning needle and push the needle through the tassel, **once above** and **once below** the binding, in opposite directions. Finally go down through the binding, incorporating the tails into the tassel. Trim the ends.

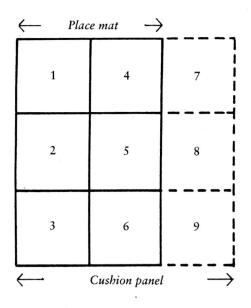

$\leftarrow$ *Place mat* $\rightarrow$

1	4	7
2	5	8
3	6	9

$\leftarrow$ *Cushion panel* $\rightarrow$

DIAGRAM 4
Sewing order for the place mat and for the cushion appliqué panel

ALTERNATIVE DOUBLE CHAIN. Cut a length of cotton 35 in approx. Thread through the suggested point on the pattern, under a double thread if possible. Pull till the cut ends are of even length. Tie a single knot close to the work. Insert the hook in the same place and pull one of the cotton threads through. Work required length of chs, and add the tassel as described above. Insert hook again and catch the remaining thread, working a second chain, the same length as the first. Add a tassel as before. Trim.

Opposite. Sugar starch bowl with a curved edge, see page 28.

SUGAR STARCH BOWL

Approximate sizes: Bowl with curved edge (previous page), diameter: 6½ in, depth: 2 in. Bowl with straight sides (see page 31), diameter: 5½ in, depth 2½ in

MATERIALS. Small quantity, (less than 1 oz / 25 g), pale yellow bedspread-weight cotton thread / No 10, a No 7 / 1.50 mm crochet hook

TENSION / GAUGE. The diameter of round 1 should measure ¾ in

WORKING NOTES
- ch3 at beginning of each round count as 1dc.
- Change direction each round. **From round 11,** do not turn.
- If unsure where to place the sl st at the end of each round, **mark 3rd of ch-3** at beginning of round with a safety pin, removing and replacing it at the start of each round. Correct placing of sl st produces an almost invisible seam on the bowl.
- It is also important to have the correct number of stitches on each round as it is easier to count them **before** you link with a sl st. Adjust the number if necessary, before continuing.
- For sugar starching, see method on page 30.
- Refer to the diagram opposite as you work.

BEGIN. (See diagram opposite.) ch5, sl st to form a ring.

Round 1   ch3, 14dc into ring (15sts incl ch-3), sl st to 3rd of ch3, turn.

Round 2   ch3, 1dc at the base of ch-3, *2dc together in each st, repeat from* till the end of the round (30sts incl ch-3), sl st to 3rd of ch-3, turn.

Round 3   ch3, 1dc at the base of ch-3, 1dc in next st, *2dc together in next st, 1dc in next st, repeat from* till the end of the round (45sts including ch-3), sl st to 3rd of ch-3, turn.

Round 4   ch3, 1dc at the base of ch-3, *1dc in each next 2sts, 2dc together in next st, repeat from* till the end of the round. End with 1dc in each last 2sts (60sts including ch-3), sl st to the 3rd of ch-3, turn.

Round 5   ch3, 1dc at the base of ch-3, *1dc in each next 3sts, 2dc together in next st, repeat from* till the end of the round. End with 1dc in each last 3sts (75sts incl ch-3), sl st to 3rd of ch-3, turn.

Round 6   ch3, 1dc in next st, **not** st at the base of ch-, 1dc in each st till the end of the round (75sts including ch-3) sl st to the 3rd of ch-3, turn.

Over the next few rounds, your work will begin to curve into a bowl shape.

Round 7   ch3, 1dc at the base of ch-3, *1dc in each next 5sts, 2dc together in next st, repeat from* till the end of the round. End with 1dc in each last 2sts, after last 2dc together (88 sts), sl st to the 3rd of ch-3, turn.

The sequence of sts will not work out exactly from round 7. Check diagram.

DIAGRAM **1**

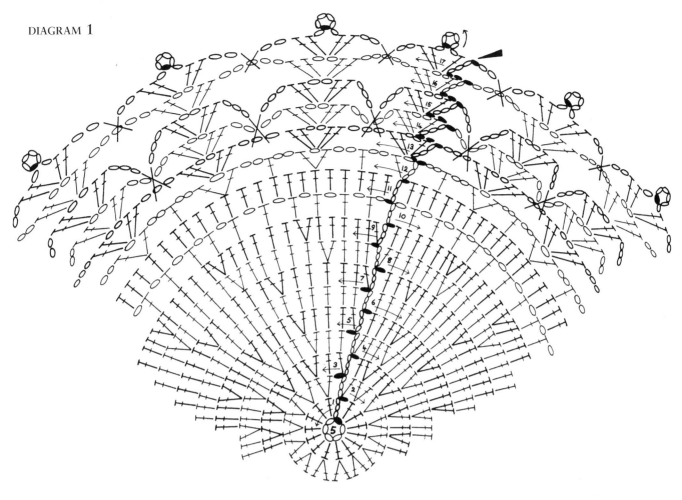

Right side

Round 8. ch3, 1dc at base of ch-3, *1dc in each next 5sts, 2dc together in next st, repeat from* till the end of the round. End with 1dc in each last 3sts, after last 2dc together (103sts), sl st to the 3rd of ch-3, turn.

Round 9 ch3, 1dc at the base of ch-3, *1dc in each next 5sts, 2dc together in next st, repeat from* till the end of the round. End with 1dc in each last 6sts, after last 2dc together (120sts), sl st to the 3rd of ch-3, turn.

Round 10 ch4, skip st at the base of ch-4 **and** next st, 1dc in next st, *ch1, skip a st, 1dc in next st, repeat from* till the end of the round. End with ch1 and a sl st to 3rd of ch-4 (60sps), turn.

Round 11 ch3, 1dc in first sp, *1dc in next st, 1dc in next sp, repeat from* till the end of the round (120sts), sl st to the 3rd of ch-3.

From round 11 Do not turn. Work in the same direction till the pattern is complete. Check number of sts and adjust if necessary.

Round 12 ch4, 1dc at the base of ch-4, *ch2, skip 2sts, 1dc in the next st, ch2, skip 2sts, (1dc, ch1, 1dc) in next st, repeat from* till the end of the round. End with ch2, skip 2sts, 1dc in the next st, ch2, skip 2sts, sl st to the 3rd of ch-4, sl st **again** into ch-1 sp.

Round 13 ch3, (1dc, ch2, 2dc) in the first ch-1

sp, *ch3, skip 2ch, 1dc, ch2. Work (2dc, ch2, 2dc) in next ch-1 sp, repeat from* till the end of the round. End with ch3, sl st to the 3rd of ch-3, sl st in the next dc **and again** into ch1 sp.

Round 14 ch3, (1dc, ch2, 2dc) in the first ch-2 sp *ch4, (2dc, ch2, 2dc) in next ch-2 sp, repeat from* till the end of the round. End with ch4, sl st to the 3rd of ch-3, sl st in the next dc **and again** into ch-2 sp.

Round 15 ch3, (1dc, ch2, 2dc) in the first ch-2 sp, *ch3, work a tight sc around the ch-4 on round 14 and ch-3 on round 13, pulling the chains together (see diagram on page 29). ch3 (2dc, ch2, 2dc) in the next ch-2 sp, repeat from* till the end of the round. End with ch3, sl st to the 3rd of ch-3, sl st in the next dc **and again** in the ch-1 sp.

Round 16 ch3, (1dc, ch2, 2dc) in first ch-2 sp, *ch5, (2dc, ch2, 2dc) in next ch-2 sp, repeat from* till the end of the round. End with ch5, and a sl st to the 3rd of ch-3, sl st in next dc **and again** in the ch-1 sp.

Round 17 ch3, 1dc in ch-2 sp, (ch1, 1 x ch4 picot, ch1, 2dc) in same ch-2 sp, *ch2, 1 tight sc around ch-5 on round 16, ch2, (2dc, ch1, 1 x ch4 picot, ch1, 2dc) in next ch-2 sp, repeat from* till the end of the round. End with ch2, 1 tight sc around ch-5, ch2, sl st to the 3rd of ch-3. Finish off, weave in ends.

SUGAR STARCHING

Use this traditional method to stiffen a piece of work so that it can be used as a free-standing object, such as the bowls featured here. The same method can be used to starch small suitable motifs to produce the components of a mobile or to make Christmas tree decorations.

MATERIALS. Half a cup of granulated sugar, half a cup of water, a plain glass bowl to use as a mould for the crochet shape (up to 6 in in diameter). A large plate or tray on which to stand the glass bowl while the crochet is wet.

METHOD. Mix sugar and water in a small pan, place over a low heat. Stir till sugar is completely dissolved, using a wooden spoon. Do not allow to boil. Remove from heat and allow to cool. Soak the piece of crochet thoroughly in the sugar solution and squeeze out the excess liquid gently.

STRAIGHT-SIDED BOWL (see opposite)
Turn glass bowl upside down and carefully fit the lace over the bowl. Center the base of the work as accurately as you can. Smooth the sides of the work over the bowl and gently pull out the picots, to the same length and spacing all round. Allow to dry for at least 24 hours. Then ease a palette knife between the glass bowl and the crochet but do not remove. Allow to dry for at least another 12 hours. Carefully remove the work from its glass mould.

BOWL WITH CURVED EDGE (see page 27)
Starch as explained above. After a few hours, and when the crochet begins to stiffen, gently bend the last two rows of crochet outward, as evenly as possible. Before the work hardens fully, check that you are fully satisfied with the edge and adjust it if necessary. Once completely dry, sew or glue tiny pearls at the tip of each point. In a damp atmosphere, the starched object can become sticky. To prevent this, spray the finished article with a studio preservative spray. If dirty, wash the object in plenty of warm soapy water, rinsing it well in clear water. Dry fully and starch again.

Opposite. Straight-sided sugar starch bowl.

SQUARE PIN CUSHION

Approximate size: 3 in square

MATERIALS. 1 oz / 25 g pale yellow or white bedspread-weight cotton thread / No 10, a No 7 / 1.50 mm crochet hook, a scrap of silk or cotton fabric to cover the cushion pad, a small amount of polyester batting

TENSION / GAUGE

 = 4sps

← 1 in →

WORKING NOTES

◆ The panel consists entirely of open mesh filet, with 2ch between the dcs.

BEGIN. ch41 (see diagram 1)

DIAGRAM 1

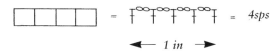

3

2 →

ch41 (12sps)

Row 1   1dc in 8th ch from hook, *work ch2, skip 2ch, 1dc in next ch, repeat from* to the end of the row, (12 x ch-2 sps), ch5, turn.

Row 2   Skip 2ch, 1dc in the next dc, *ch2, skip 2ch, 1dc in next dc, repeat from* to the end of the row. Finish with ch2, skip 2ch, 1dc in next ch, ch5, turn.

Row 3   As row 2. Repeat till 13 rows from the start. Do not turn, do not cut the thread.

DECREASING EDGE

Round 1   ch2, 2sc in the corner sp, 2sc in each of the following ch sps, 5sc in corner sp, continue in the same way until you reach the starting corner sp, 2sc in this sp, sl st to ch-2 to complete the round. Do not cut the thread, hold the loop with a safety pin.

At this stage, you should make the inner cloth cover for the pad. Cut 2 pieces of fabric, ½ in bigger than the crochet square to allow for the seams. With right sides together, stitch around, leaving an opening along the fourth side. Turn out and fill with batting, pushing it well into the corners. Close the opening.

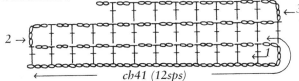

This pattern can also be used to produce a lavender sachet. Proceed exactly as described, but replace the batting with lavender or potpourri (see page 49), where such a square sachet is shown, together with a round one). These small projects are quick and easy to work, yet make delightful presents.

DECREASING EDGE (continued)

Having completed the inner pad cover, you can resume the work to form the back of the crochet cover. Remove the safety pin from the corner of the crochet panel and work ch3. The next 4 rounds must be worked very firmly.

Round 2 1dc in each sc on all 4 sides of the mesh square. The work should now begin to curve inwards to form a casing for the cushion pad. End with a sl st to 3rd of ch3 at the beginning of the round, ch-3, turn.

Round 3 Decrease next 2dc, *1dc in each next 2sts, decrease next 2dc, repeat from*. End with a sl st to ch3 at beginning of the round, ch3, turn.

Round 4 Decrease next 2dc, *1dc in each next 3sts, decrease 2dc, repeat from*. End with a sl st to the ch-3 at the beginning of the round, ch3, turn.

Round 5 1dc in each stitch till the end of the round. By now, the edge of the work should be sufficiently curved to achieve a snug fit on the cushion pad. If not, repeat round 5, decreasing 2dc every 8th or 10th st till the end of the round, sl st to the 3rd of ch-3 at the beginning of the round. Finish off, weave in ends.

PICOT EDGING

With the right side of the work facing you, join the thread by tying it once around the stem/post (see diagram 2) of a corner dc, on the last row

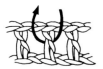

DIAGRAM 2
stem or post - (the vertical part of the stitch)

of the mesh panel, ch3, *1sc around stem/post of the next dc, ch3, repeat from* working ch3 at the corners till the end of the round. End with a sl st to the first of ch-3 at the beginning of the

round. **Do not turn.** ch2 (to count as 1sc), (1sc, 1 x ch4 picot, 1sc) in the first ch-3 loop and in each ch-3 loop until the round is complete. End with a sl st to the 2nd of ch-2 at the beginning of the round, work ch25 (firmly), sl st to base of ch-25. Turn and work 30sc in ch-25 loop, sl st to first sc. This completes the loop from which to hang the pin cushion. Finish off, weave in ends. Ease the cover over the prepared pad.

Below: This romantic square pin cushion is based on a popular Victorian design, which forms part of the collection shown on page 33.

VICTORIAN PIN CUSHION

Approximate size, including frill: 5¼ x 6 in

MATERIALS. 1 oz / 25 g white bedspread-weight cotton thread / No 10, a No 7 / 1.50 mm crochet hook, a scrap of silk or cotton fabric to cover the pad, a small amount of polyester batting, 36 in of narrow ribbon

STITCHES, ABBREVIATIONS & SYMBOLS

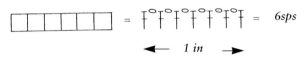

TENSION / GAUGE

WORKING NOTES
♦ ch1 between dcs on open mesh
♦ Refer to diagram opposite as you work.

BEGIN. ch46

Row 1 1dc in 6th ch from hook, *ch1, skip 1ch, 1dc in next ch, repeat from* to the end. End with 1dc in last ch st (21sps), ch4, turn.

Row 2 Skip 1ch, 1dc in dc, *ch1, skip 1ch, 1dc in dc, repeat from* till 6sps made. Work 1dc in sp, 1dc in dc (last 3dcs make 1 block), (see diagram 1). Continue, following the diagram and working the blocks and spaces to complete the star design (21 rows). **Do not finish off.** ch2,

work 2sc (firmly) into every ch-1 sp around the edge of the filet pattern, adding an extra 2sc in the corner sps. End with a sl st to the 2nd of ch-2. **Do not finish off**. Hold the loop with a safety pin.

At this stage, cut 2 pieces of fabric, ½ in larger all round than the crochet panel to allow for the seams. Stitch the 2 pieces, right sides together, leaving a gap along one side to turn the work.

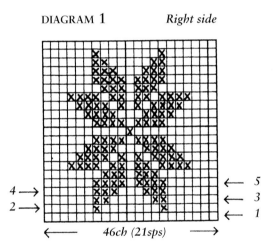

DIAGRAM **1**   *Right side*

46ch (21sps)

Turn out, fill with batting till quite firm, making sure it goes right into the corners. Slip-stitch the opening.

TO COMPLETE THE CROCHET COVER
Remove the safety pin from the working loop (see diagram 2, page 36).

Round 1 ch3, dec 2dc, *1dc in next st, dec 2dc, rep from* till round all 4 sides, a sl st to the 3rd of ch-3 to complete the round. ch3, do not turn.

Round 2 Decrease next 2dc, *1dc in each st till

DIAGRAM 2

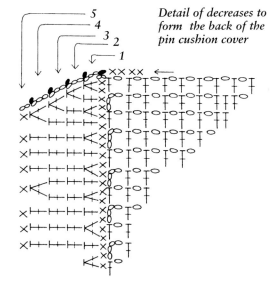

Detail of decreases to form the back of the pin cushion cover

FRILL

Join the thread by tying it around the stem or post of a dc, at one of the corners of the front panel (see diagram 3). *ch3, 1sc around stem of next dc, repeat from* till you reach the **first** ch-3 loop, 1sc in that loop, *ch5, 1sc in next ch-3 loop, repeat from* till you reach the **first** ch-5 loop, repeat from* till you reach the **first** ch-7 loop, 1sc in that loop. If you wish to have a fuller frill, add another round of ch-7 loops. Cut the thread and finish off. Weave in ends.

DIAGRAM 3
Stem or post (the vertical part of the stitch)

you reach the next corner, decrease 3dc at corner, repeat from* till round. End with a sl st to the 3rd of ch-3, ch3, do not turn. The mesh panel should now begin to curve inwards to form a casing, if not, check the tension and, if necessary, rework round 2, using a smaller hook. Then continue as follows:

Round 3 As round 2, but decrease 2dc at the corners. End with a sl st to the 3rd of ch-3, ch3, do not turn.

Check the fit again. **If too loose**, repeat round 2, decrease 2dc at the corners **and** decrease 2 or 3dc together at the center of each side. Check the fit once again, then continue:

Round 4 Decrease next 2dc, *1dc in each of next 3sts, dec 2dc, repeat from* till the end of the round, sl st to the 3rd of ch-3, ch2, do not turn.

Round 5 1sc in each st, work firmly to obtain a firm edge. This last round can be repeated if the cover is still a little loose. Finish off, weave in ends.

TO COMPLETE

Cut the ribbon into 2 equal lengths. Start threading it at one corner, on the last round of the main panel, just before the first round of the frill. Continue threading the ribbon over and under the stem or post of dcs, until half way round, finishing at one corner. Thread the other length of ribbon through the remaining 2 edges. Even up tail ends, tie in small neat bows in the 2 corners, trim.

IRISH ROSE PIN CUSHION

Approximate size (including the frill): 4½ in in diameter

MATERIALS. 1 oz / 25g (or remnant) white bedspread-weight cotton thread / No 10 , a No 7 / 1.50 mm crochet hook, a scrap of silk or cotton fabric to cover the pad, a small amount of polyester batting

WORKING NOTES
♦ Refer to the diagrams on page 38 as you work.
♦ Note the special ending on rounds 2 to 7.
♦ It may help to mark the first ch loop of each round. Remove and replace the marker as you work.

BEGIN. ch7, sl st to form a ring (see diagram 1).

Round 1 ch1, 12sc in ring, sl st to first sc. **Do not turn** on this or any of the following rounds.

Round 2 ch3, skip 1sc, 1sc in next st *ch3, 1sc in the next sc, repeat from*. End with ch1, 1hdc in the first sc.

Round 3 ch4, 1sc in ch-3 sp, *ch4, 1sc in the next ch-3 sp, repeat from*. End with ch1, 1dc in hdc of previous round.

Round 4 *ch5, 1sc in ch-4 sp, repeat from*. End with ch2, 1dc in dc of previous round. Continue, following diagram 1, until you **complete round 9. Take note** of the number of ch sts and of the stitch used to complete each round.

Round 9 Should have 66 x ch-1 sps (adjust to correct number of sps, if necessary). Do not finish off. Hold the loop with a safety pin.

At this stage, cut 2 pieces of material ½ in larger all round than the crochet panel. Stitch together, right sides facing, leaving a gap to insert the pad. Turn out. Fill with batting, pushing it well into the corners. Close the opening.

TO COMPLETE THE BACK OF THE COVER
Remove the safety pin and decrease as follows:

Round 10 ch2, (1hdc, ch1 in each ch-1 sp) till the end of the round, sl st to ch-2. **Do not turn.**

Round 11 ch2, 1hdc in first hdc, *skip 1ch, 1hdc in next hdc, repeat from* till the end of the round, sl st to ch-2.

Round 12 ch2, 1hdc in each next 4sts, *decrease 2hdc, 1hdc in each next 4sts, repeat from* till the end of the round, sl st to ch-2. (The sequence of sts may not work out exactly on this round.)

Round 13 ch2, 1hdc in each st (work firmly), sl st to ch-2. Try the cover on the pad. **If it is a little loose, add an extra round of tightly worked sc.** Finish off, weave in ends.

DECORATIVE FRILL
Round 1 Tie thread around the stem or post of any dc on round 9 (see diagram 2). Work ch4, *1sc around stem of next dc, ch4, repeat from* till the end of the round. End with ch4

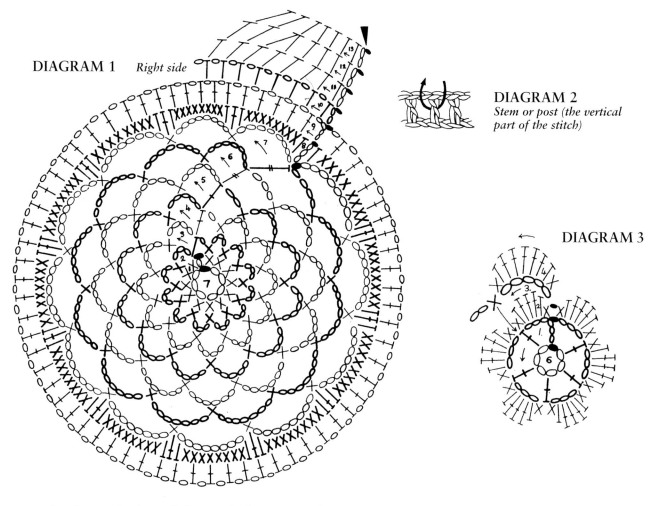

DIAGRAM 1 *Right side*

DIAGRAM 2
Stem or post (the vertical part of the stitch)

DIAGRAM 3

and a sl st to the first of ch-4 at the beginning of the round.

Round 2 sl st in next ch st, ch5, *1sc in next ch-4 sp, ch5, repeat from*. End with ch5, and a sl st to the first of ch-5 at the beginning of the round.

Round 3 sl st in each next ch2 sts, ch5, 1sc in 1st ch5 sp *(ch5, 1sc, ch5, 1sc) in next ch5 sp, repeat from* till the end of round. End with ch5, sl st to 1st of ch5 at the beginning of the round. Finish off, weave in ends.

IRISH ROSE MOTIF (see diagram 3)

BEGIN. ch6, sl st to form a ring,

Round 1 ch6, 1dc in ring, *ch3, 1dc in ring, repeat from* till the 5th sp. End with ch3, sl st to

3rd of ch-6, making 6sps altogether. Do not turn.

Round 2 (1sc, 1hdc, 3dc, 1hdc, 1sc) in first ch-3 sp, and in each ch-3 sp till the end of the round, sl st to the first sc (6 petals). Do not turn.

Round 3 Work ch5 behind first petal, 1sc in dc on round 1 (between 2scs), *ch5 behind the next petal, 1sc in next dc, repeat from* till 6 x ch-5 loops, sl st to first of ch-5 at beginning of the round. Do not turn.

Round 4 (1sc, 1hdc, 5dc, 1hdc, 1sc) in each of 6 loops, sl st to sc at the beginning of the round. Finish off, weave in ends.

Attach the rose to the center of the prepared cover. Slip it over the pad. Your Irish rose pin cushion is now ready.

To make a smaller version of the rose pin cushion, or to produce covers for guest soaps, as shown on this page, use bedspread-weight cotton thread / No 20, with a No. 8 / 1.25 mm crochet hook.

TEA TRAY CLOTH

Approximate size: 18 x 12 in

MATERIALS. 4 oz / 100 g white bedspread-weight cotton thread / No 10, a No 7 / 1.50 mm crochet hook

STITCHES, ABBREVIATIONS & SYMBOLS

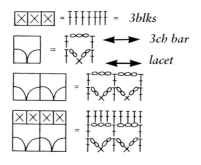

TENSION / GAUGE

DIAGRAM 1 *Right side*

For instructions on finishing the edge, see diagram 2, on page 42.

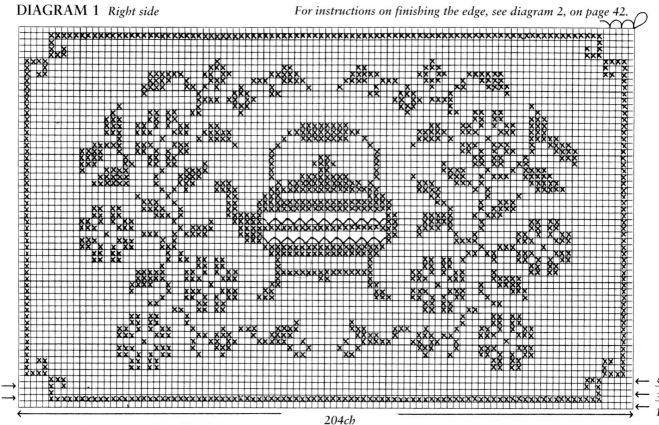

4 →
2 →

← 5
← 3
← 1

204ch
(100sps)

WORKING NOTES
♦ ch1 between dcs on open mesh
♦ You may may find it useful to color in each row on a photocopy of the diagram, as the work proceeds.

BEGIN. ch204

Row 1   1dc in 6th ch from hook, *ch1, skip 1ch, 1dc in next ch, repeat from* to the end (100sps), ch4, turn.

Row 2   Skip 1ch, 1dc in next dc, *ch1, skip 1ch, 1dc in next dc, repeat from* till 5sps made, 1dc in next sp, 1dc in next dc (1 block). Continue this row as shown on diagram 1. End with 5sps, ch4, turn.

Continue, following diagram 1, working blocks and spaces to a firm even tension, till you reach row 60 (top right hand-corner of panel). **Do not finish off.**

FINISHED EDGE (see diagram 2)
With the right side of the work facing you, work ch8 (tightly), 1sc into st at the base of the ch-8 (1 corner loop made). *Work ch5, skip 2sps, 1sc in next dc, repeat from* till you reach the next corner, work ch8, 1sc beside last sc, 2nd corner loop is made). *Work ch5, skip 2sps, 1sc in dc (opposite the end of the row). Repeat from* till the next corner point, work ch8, 1sc beside last sc. *Work ch5, skip 2sps, 1sc in next dc, repeat from* along lower edge. Continue till you have worked all 4 edges. End with a sl st at the base of the first ch-8 loop. **Do not turn,** continue in the same direction, working firmly. *7sc in ch-8 loop, 4sc in each ch-5 loop till you reach next ch-8 loop, repeat from* on all 4 sides. End with a sl st to first sc at the beginning of the round. Finish off, weave in tail ends.

TO COMPLETE
Press lightly on the wrong side, using a damp cloth. Ease gently into shape. If necessary, pin on a board covered with plastic wrap and allow to dry fully.

Detail of finished edge

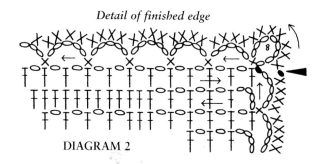

DIAGRAM 2

LACY JEWELRY CUSHION

Approximate size of panel: 5 in

MATERIALS. Remnant of white bedspread-weight cotton thread / No 10, a No 7 / 1.50 mm crochet hook, a 8 in square cushion pad, 20 in of raw silk or other fabric for the cover

SPECIAL STITCHES (see page 13)

 = *5 loop puff st*

 = *double puff st group*

TENSION / GAUGE
The diameter of rounds 1 and 2 should measure 1¼ in / 3 cm.

WORKING NOTES
◆   Work to a firm, even tension and refer to the diagram on page 45 throughout.

BEGIN. ch8, sl st to form a ring.

Round 1   ch3 (to count as a dc), 2dc in ring, ch4, *3dc in ring, ch4, repeat from* 2 more times, sl st to 3rd of ch-3. **Do not turn on this or any of the following rounds.**

Round 2   ch3, 1dc in each next 2dcs, *(3dc, ch3, 3dc) in corner sp, 1dc in each next 3dc, repeat from* 2 more times. End with (3dc, ch3, 3dc) in last corner sp. Sl st to 3rd of ch-3, sl st again into next dc.

Round 3   ch3 (to count as 1dc), 6dc at the base of ch-3, making a 7dc group. *ch3, 1 double puff st group in the corner loop, ch3, skip 4dc, 7dc in next dc, skip 4dc, repeat from* 2 more times. End with ch3, 1 double puff st group in the last corner, ch3, sl st to 3rd of ch-3.

Round 4   ch6 (to count as 1trc and ch-2), 1trc in next dc, *ch2, 1 trc in next dc, repeat from* 4 more times, (6 x ch2 sps between trcs), ch3, skip 3ch, 1 double puff st group in the next ch-2 corner sp, ch3, skip 3ch, 1trc in first dc, *ch2, 1trc in next dc, repeat from* 5 more times, ch3, skip 3ch, 1 double puff st group in the next ch-2 corner sp. Repeat st sequence, 2 more times (see diagram on page 45). End with a sl st to the 4th of ch-6, sl st again in the next ch st.

Note: Mark the first of the ch-4 from the 5th round onwards as a guide to the beginning and the end of each round. Remove and replace the marker as you work.

Round 5   *ch4, 1sc in next ch-2 sp, repeat from* 4 more times (5 loops), ch5, skip 3ch, 1 double puff st group in next ch-2 corner sp, ch5, skip 3ch, 1sc in next ch-2 sp. Repeat st sequence till the end of the round. End with ch5, sl st to the first of ch-4 (marked, see above). Sl st again in the next ch st.

Round 6   *ch4, 1sc in next ch-4 loop, repeat from* 3 more times (4 loops), ch7, skip 5ch, 1 double puff st group in ch-2 corner sp, ch7, skip 5ch, 1sc in next ch-4 loop. Repeat st sequence till the end of the round. End with ch7, sl st to first of ch-4 (marked), sl st again in the next ch st.

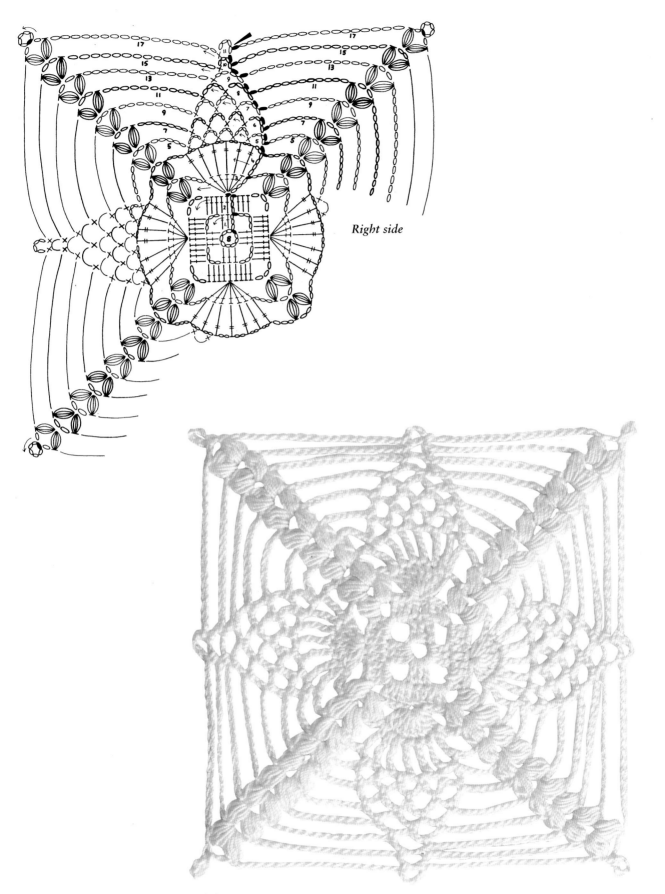

Right side

The crochet motif, shown life-size.

Round 7 *ch4, 1sc in next ch-4 loop, repeat from* 2 more times (3 loops), ch9, skip 7ch, 1 double puff st group in the ch-2 corner sp, ch9, skip 7ch, 1sc in next ch-4 loop. Repeat the st sequence till the end of the round. End with ch9, sl st to the first of ch-4, (marked). Sl st again in next ch st.

Round 8 ch4, 1sc in next loop, ch4, 1sc in next loop (2 loops), ch11, skip 9ch, 1 double puff st group in the ch-2 corner sp, ch11, skip 9ch, 1sc in next ch-4 loop. Repeat the st sequence till the end of the round. End with ch11, sl st to the first of ch-4, sl st again in the next ch st.

Round 9 ch4, 1sc in next loop, *ch13, skip 11ch, 1 double puff st group in ch-2 corner sp, ch13, skip 11ch, 1sc in next ch-4 loop, ch4, 1sc in next ch-4 loop. Repeat the st sequence from* till the end of the round. End with ch13, sl st to first of ch-4. Sl st again in the next ch st.

Round 10 ch4, 1sc back in same loop, *ch15, skip 13ch, 1 double puff st group in ch-2 corner sp, ch15, skip 13ch (1sc, ch4, 1sc) in ch-4 loop. Repeat the st sequence from* till the end of the round. End with ch15, sl st to first of ch-4. Sl st again in the next ch st.

Round 11 ch4, 1sc back in same loop, ch17, skip 15ch, *(1 x 5 loop puff st, ch1, 1 x ch5 picot, ch1, 1 x 5 loop puff st) in ch-2 corner sp, ch17, skip 15ch, (1sc, ch4, 1sc) in next ch-4 loop, ch17, skip 15ch, repeat the st sequence from*. End with ch17 after the last corner and sl st to first of ch-4. Finish off, weave in ends.

TO COMPLETE

Press lightly on the wrong side of the work, using a damp cloth. Ease into shape by pulling gently at the corners. Pin out evenly on a flat board covered in plastic wrap. Open out the picots. Leave to dry. Attach the motif in the center of the jewelry cushion with a few stitches or with pearl-headed pins, as shown in the photograph on page 44. This makes it easier to remove the lace panel and wash it.

MAKING UP THE CUSHION

Cut 2 pieces of silk, or other fabric, measuring 7½ in square (this includes a ½ in seam allowance all round). For the frill, cut a strip 3¼ in wide. To save fabric, several strips can be cut and joined to obtain a total length of 72 in. Join the 2 ends of the frill to form a ring. Press and open out the seams. Right side uppermost, fold the strip in half, lengthwise, and press flat. Gather the edge to fit around the perimeter of the cushion. Pin the frill around one of the fabric squares and machine-stitch. Put the work down on the table with the frill uppermost. Pin the second square of fabric on top of it and machine-stitch, leaving a 3½ in gap in the center of one of the sides to turn the work. Press. Fit the pad inside the cover and slip-stitch the opening.

LAVENDER SACHET

Approximate diameter: 5 in

MATERIALS. 1 oz / 25 g pale yellow bedspread-weight cotton thread / No 10, a No 7 / 1.50 mm crochet hook, a handful of lavender, a scrap of lightweight fabric for the inner pouch, 20 in of narrow ribbon

WORKING NOTES

♦ Always work in the same direction, firmly and evenly, and refer to diagram on page 48 throughout.

FRONT OF THE SACHET

BEGIN. ch6, sl st to form a ring.

Round 1 ch5 (to count as 1dc and ch-2), (1dc, ch2 in ring) 7 times, sl st to the 3rd of ch-5 (8 x ch-2 sps).

Round 2 sl st again in first ch-2 sp, ch3, 2dc in sp beside ch-3, ch2, *3dc in next ch-2 sp, ch2, repeat from* in each ch-2 sp till the end of the round. End with a sl st to 3rd of ch-3 at the beginning of the round (8 x 3dc groups and 8 x ch-2 sps).

Round 3 ch3, 1dc at base of ch-3, 1dc in next dc, 2dc together in last dc of 3dc group, ch2, skip 2ch, *2dc together in next dc, 1dc in next dc, 2dc together in last dc of 3dc group, ch2, skip 2ch, repeat from* till the end of the round. End with a sl st to the 3rd of ch-3.

Round 4 ch3 (to count as first dc), 1dc in each next 4dc, ch2, 1dc in ch-2 sp, ch2, *1dc in each next 5dc, ch2, 1dc in ch-2 sp, ch2, repeat from* till the end of the round, sl st to 3rd of ch-3.

Round 5 ch3, 1dc in next dc, decrease next 2dc, 1dc in next dc, ch2, 1dc in ch-2 sp, ch2, 1dc in dc, ch2, 1dc in next sp, ch2, *1dc in each next 2dc, dec next 2dc, 1dc in next dc, ch2, 1dc in ch-2 sp, 1dc in dc, ch2, 1dc in next sp, ch2, repeat from* till the end of the round, sl st to the 3rd of ch-3.

Round 6 ch3, decrease next 2dc, 1dc in next dc, (ch2, 1dc in ch-2 sp) 4 times, ch2, *1dc in next dc, decrease next 2dc, 1dc in next dc, (ch2, 1dc in ch-2 sp) 4 times, ch2, repeat from* till the end of the round, sl st to 3rd of ch-3.

Round 7 sl st again in next st, ch5, skip 1dc, *(1dc in ch-2 sp, ch2) in each next 5sps, ch2, skip 1dc, 1dc in next st, skip 1dc, ch2, repeat from* till the end of the round, sl st to the 3rd of ch-5 (48 sps).

Round 8 Work this round slightly tighter. ch1, *3sc in next ch-2 sp, repeat from* till the end of the round, sl st to the first sc at the beginning of the round.

Round 9 ch5, skip 1 st, 1dc in next st, ch2, *skip 1 st, 1dc in next st, repeat from* till the end of the round, sl st to the 3rd of ch5 (72 sps). It is important to have the correct number of spaces on this round.

Round 10 sl st again in the first ch-2 sp, ch5, 1dc in same sp as ch-5, ch1, 1sc in next ch-2 sp, ch1, *(1dc, ch2, 1dc) in next ch-2 sp, ch1, 1sc in next ch-2 sp, ch1, repeat from* till the end of the round, sl st to 3rd of ch-5.

Round 11   sl st again in first ch sp, ch3, (3dc, 1 x ch4 picot, 4dc) in same sp as ch-3, 1sc in next ch-2 sp *(4dc, 1 x ch4 picot, 4dc) in next ch-2 sp, 1sc in next ch-2 sp, repeat from* till the end of the round, sl st to the 3rd of ch-3. Finish off, weave in ends.

BACK OF THE SACHET
Proceed exactly as for the front panel, but omit rounds 10 and 11.

INNER POUCH
Cut 2 circles of fabric, ½ in larger than the back section of the sachet. Sew the pieces together leaving a small opening to turn the work. Fill the pouch with lavender (do not overfill). Close the opening with a few slip stitches.

ASSEMBLING THE SACHET
Overlap the 2 pieces of crochet, wrong sides together, and carefully thread the narrow ribbon in and out of round 9 to join the 2 layers. Leave a gap through which to insert the lavender bag. When this is done, continue weaving the ribbon. Tie a neat bow on the front of the sachet.

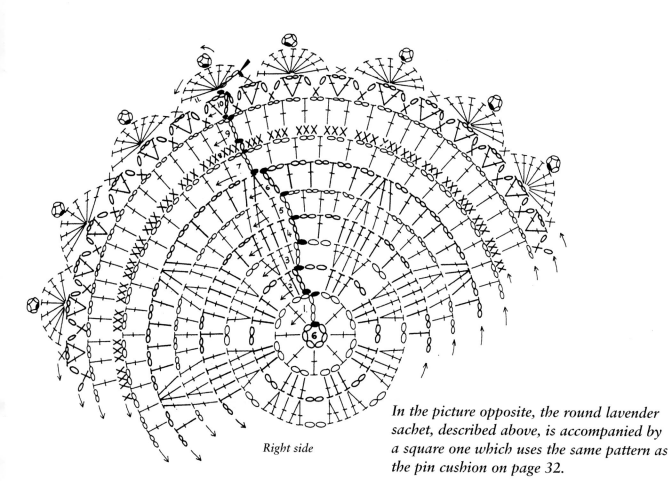

Right side

In the picture opposite, the round lavender sachet, described above, is accompanied by a square one which uses the same pattern as the pin cushion on page 32.

LUCKY STAR CUSHION

Approximate size of the cushion (excluding the frill): 12 in square

MATERIALS. 4 oz / 100 g white bedspread-weight cotton thread / No 10 , a No 7 / 1.50 mm crochet hook, 1 cushion pad 12 in square, white or contrasting silk or other fabric to cover the cushion pad, 110 in narrow ribbon, decorative bow (optional)

STITCHES, ABBREVIATIONS & SYMBOLS

☐ = 𝆑°𝆑 = *1sp*

☒ = 𝆑𝆑𝆑 = *1blk*

☐☒☒☐ = 𝆑°𝆑𝆑𝆑𝆑𝆑°𝆑 = *1sp, 2blks, 1sp*

TENSION / GAUGE

 = 𝆑°𝆑°𝆑°𝆑°𝆑°𝆑°𝆑 = *6sps*

← 1 in →

CHECKING THE TENSION

The length of the first row should be no less than 12 in and no more than 13 in. If too tight, use a bigger hook, if too loose, use a smaller hook.

WORKING NOTES

♦ ch1 between dcs on open mesh
♦ Make a photocopy of the diagram on page 52.

BEGIN. ch135, fairly tight and even.

Row 1 1dc in 6th ch from hook. *ch1, skip 1ch, 1dc in next ch, repeat from* to the end of of the row (65sps), ch4, turn. **Important.** Check the tension and the length of the first row before continuing.

Row 2 Skip 1ch sp, 1dc in dc, *ch1, skip 1ch sp, 1dc in dc, repeat from* to end, ch4, turn.

Row 3 as row 2

Now follow the diagram, working blocks and spaces to form the design until you reach the half-way point, then turn the prepared photocopy upside down and proceed with the second half of the design (65 rows). **Do not finish off.**

DECORATIVE FRILL (front panel only)
ch5, 1sc in first sp, mark this first loop with a safety pin, ch5, 1sc in next sp, work all around the edge of the panel, working an extra loop in corner sps, till you reach the marked loop. *Remove marker pin. Work ch5, 1sc in that loop, replace the pin in the completed loop, and continue, working ch5, 1sc in the next loop till you reach the marked loop. Repeat from* till 7 rounds are complete. Finish off, weave in tail ends. For a fuller frill, add 1 or 2 extra rounds.

TO COMPLETE THE COVER
The star design can be repeated on the back of the cushion, or substituted by a plain filet crochet mesh: 1dc, ch1, 1dc worked over the 135ch (65sps) and for 65 rows. Finish off, weave in all tail ends. Press both sections lightly, using a damp cloth, ease into shape. Pin out to correct size if necessary.

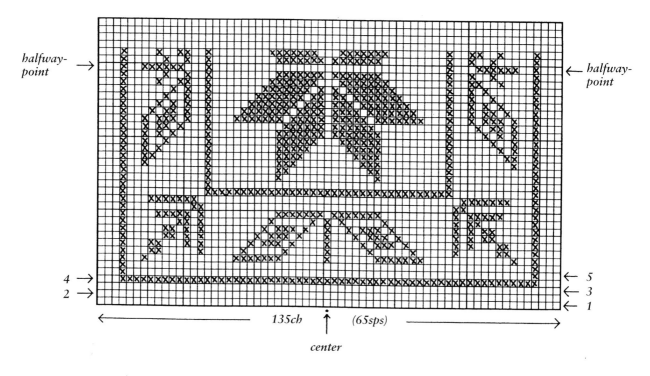

halfway-point →

← *halfway-point*

4 →
2 →

← 5
← 3
← 1

135ch   (65sps)

center

ASSEMBLING THE CUSHION

Make up the fabric cover by cutting 2 squares of the selected fabric, allowing ½ in for the seams. Machine-stitch, leaving a 6 in gap to turn out the work. Insert pad and slip-stitch the gap.

Overlay the 2 filet crochet panels, wrong sides together, ensuring that the spaces in the filet are aligned. Cut the ribbon in half and thread one length through the outer edges of the first 2 sides, threading it over and under dcs. Start at a corner space (just before the onset of the frill). Thread the remaining ribbon through the third side and slip the prepared cushion inside the cover before threading the ribbon through the fourth side. Even out the 2 ends of the ribbon and tie in neat bows. Alternatively, a bow made with a wider ribbon can be fixed with a couple of stitches at one corner.

DAINTY BOOKMARKS

STRAIGHT BOOKMARK (see diagram opposite)

Approximate length, including tassel: 8 in

MATERIALS. Remnants of white, pale blue, pale yellow bedspread-weight cotton thread / No 10, a No 7 / 1.50 mm crochet hook

BEGIN. ch6, sl st to form a ring.

Row 1 ch3 (to count as a dc), (2dc, ch3, 3dc) in ring, **not** in ch sts, ch3, turn.

Row 2 Skip 2dc, (3dc, ch3, 3dc) in ch-3 sp, skip 2dc, 1dc in 3rd of ch-3 on row before, ch3, turn.

Row 3 Skip 3dc, (3dc, ch3, 3dc) in ch-3 sp, skip 3dc, 1dc in 3rd of ch-3 on row before, ch3, turn.

Row 4 to row 12 Work as row 3.

Row 13 Work as row 3 but omit the final ch-3, turn at the end of the row. **Do not** finish off.

Row 14 (Edging) ch2, following the diagram opposite, work along the 1st long side of the bookmark, 3sc in first sp, 3sc in next sp until you reach the end of the top edge. End with a sl st to the 2nd of ch-2 at the start of edging. Finish off, weave in ends. Complete by adding a tassel at the end of ch-12 or the alternative double ch with tassels. The instructions for tassel making are on page 26.

Note: A decorative edge worked in a contrasting color can be added if desired. Before

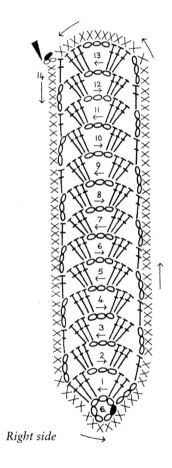

Right side →

Examples of this bookmark with, both with the plain and the contrasting edging, appear on page 54.

attaching the tassel(s), work the edge as follows: join the thread to a st beside the finishing-off point, work ch1, 1sc in each sc, with 3sc together in the center sc at the lower point of the bookmark. Use your imagination to ring the changes: the tassels can be replaced by an interesting bead or even a tiny bell.

These bookmarks, especially the straight ones, are perfect beginners' projects and yet they will make welcome gifts. The straight, as well as the cross-shaped bookmarks, can be worked with a contrasting edge.

LARGER BOOKMARK WITH A PICOT EDGE
(see photograph on page 57).

Approximate length, excluding ribbon: 5½ in

MATERIALS. Remnant of dark red bedspread weight cotton thread / No 10, a No 6 / 1.75 mm crochet hook, 12 in of ribbon

Follow the instructions for the small bookmark, as given on page 53, but work a total of 17 rows. **Do not** finish off.

Round 18   ch2, 3sc in first sp, *3sc in next sp. Repeat from* along the first long side, round the lower point of the bookmark, along the other long side and across the top edge, as shown on the diagram for the small bookmark. End with a sl st to the 2nd of ch-2 at the start of edging.

Round 19   (picot edging) Use a **No 8 / 1.25 mm** crochet hook for this last round. This will ensure a neater finish. ch5, sl st to the 3rd ch from hook (1 x ch3 picot is now made), *1sc in each next 3sc, work 1 x ch3 picot, repeat from* till the end of the round. End with 1sc in last 3sts, sl st to base of first picot. Finish off, weave in ends. Press lightly on the wrong side with a damp cloth. Slip-stitch to a length of ribbon. I used a cheerful tartan one, knotted one end and unravelled the threads to form a tassel.

CROSS-SHAPED BOOKMARK
Approximate length including tassel: 8 in

MATERIALS. Remnants of white, pale yellow or pale blue bedspread-weight cotton thread / No 10, a No 7 / 1.50 mm crochet hook

BEGIN. Following the diagram opposite, work ch12, sl st to form a ring, ch2, (12sc, ch3, 4dc, ch3, 4dc) in ring, 1dc in the 2nd of ch-2 at beginning of the round, turn.

Row 2 ch3, skip 4dc, (4dc, ch3, 4dc) in ch-3 sp, skip 3dc, 1dc in next dc, ch3, turn.

Row 3 to Row 7 Work as row 2, turn.

Row 8 Work ch15, fairly tightly, skip (4dc, ch3, 3dc), sl st in next dc, turn.

Row 9 ch3, (3dc, ch3, 8dc, ch3, 8dc, ch3, 4dc) in ch-15 sp, turn.

LEFT SECTION OF THE CROSS
Row 10 ch3, skip 3dc, (4dc, ch3, 4dc) in ch-3 sp, skip 3dc, 1dc in next dc, turn.

Row 11 ch3, skip 4dc (4dc, ch3, 4dc) in ch-3 sp, skip 3dc, 1dc in next dc. Finish off.

RIGHT SECTION OF THE CROSS
Row 12 Rejoin to 3rd of ch-3 at the beginning of row 9, work ch3, skip 3dc, (4dc, ch3, 4dc) in ch-3 sp, skip 3dc, 1dc in next dc, turn.

Row 13 ch3, skip 4dc (4dc, ch3, 4dc) in ch3 sp, skip 3dc, 1dc in next dc. Finish off.

TOP SECTION OF THE CROSS
Row 14 Rejoin at the 5th of the 8dc on row 9, work ch3, skip 3dc (4dc, ch3, 4dc) in ch-3 sp, skip 3dc, 1dc in next dc, turn.

Row 15 ch3, skip 4dc, (4dc, ch3, 4dc) in ch-3 sp, skip 3dc, 1dc in next dc, turn.

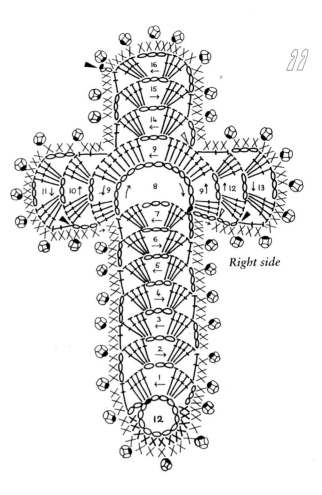

Right side

*Diagram of the cross-shaped bookmark.
As in the case of the other bookmarks, the
edging of the little cross can be worked
in a contrasting color.*

Row 16 As row 15, but **do not turn** at the end of the row. Unless you want to work a contrasting edge, **do not finish off** at this point.

PICOT EDGING
If the edge is of the same color as the cross, work down the left-hand side of the cross as follows: ch2, (3sc, 1 x ch3 picot) in first sp, (3sc, 1 x ch3 picot) in next ch-3 sp, 3sc, **no picot** in next sp, (3sc, 1 x ch3 picot) in first sp on **the left section** of the cross, (3sc, 1 x ch3 picot) in next ch3 sp, 1sc in each next 2dc, (1sc, 1 x ch3 picot) in next dc. Continue working this picot edging

all around the cross, as shown on the diagram on page 55, checking the position of the picots carefully. End with a sl st to the ch-2 at the start of edging. **Finish off** and weave in all tail ends.

CONTRASTING COLORED PICOT EDGE
Finish off at the end of row 16, join the new color to the last dc on row 16 (tie under top 2 threads). Begin with ch2 and work the picot edge as before, following the diagram carefully.

End with a sl st to the ch-2 at the start of edging. **Finish off**, weave in all tail ends.

TO COMPLETE
Chains and tassels can also be added if you wish. For the tassels, refer to page 26. Press the finished bookmark lightly, using a damp cloth, pull gently into shape and pin on a board covered with plastic wrap. Leave to dry.

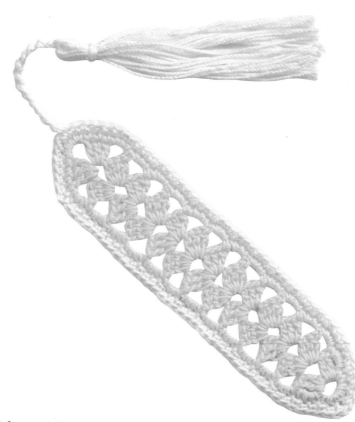

Straight bookmark with a contrasting edge

VANITY POUCH

PPP

Approximate **depth of crochet panel:** 6½ in. When mounted up the pochette is 7 in deep and is large enough to contain an average-sized compact and a lipstick, keeping your handbag neat and tidy.

MATERIALS. 1 oz / 25g bedspread-weight cotton thread / No 10, a No 7 / 1.50 mm crochet hook, a Velcro dot and 1 small button

TENSION / GAUGE
The diameter of round 1 should be ½ in

WORKING NOTES
♦ Refer to diagram opposite throughout and keep the tension firm and even.
♦ The motif is worked in the same direction on every round.
♦ Pay particular attention to the beginning and the end of each round, marking the sts where necessary.
♦ On the diagram, the **first** sc of each round is marked with a small dot up to round 13.
♦ You may find it helpful to color each round on a photocopy of the diagram, alternating 2 colors to distinguish each round.

BEGIN. ch6, sl st to form a ring.

Round 1 ch3 (to count as a dc), 11dc in ring (12sts incl ch-3), sl st to the 3rd of ch-3 to complete round. **Do not turn.**

Round 2 ch5, *skip 1dc, 1sc in next dc, ch5, repeat from* 4 more times, sl st at the base of the ch-5 at the beginning of the round (6 x ch-5 loops). **Note:** It helps to mark the first block of

3sc on the following round with a safety pin as a reminder of the beginning of each round.

Round 3 3sc in the first ch-5 loop, ch5, *3sc in next ch-5 loop, ch5, repeat from* 3 more times. End with 3sc in the last loop on this round, work 1sc in each of next 2sc, making a 5sc blk. (The completed 5sc blk marks the beginning of round 4.)

Round 4 ch5, *skip 1sc, 3sc in next loop, 1sc in each of the next 2sc, ch5, rep from* 3 more times. End with 3sc in the next loop, 1sc in each of the next 4sc, making a 7sc blk. (The completed 7sc blk marks the beginning of round 5.)

Round 5 ch5, *skip 1sc, 3sc in next loop, 1sc in each of the next 4sc, ch5, rep from* 3 more times. End with 3sc in next loop, 1sc in each of the next 6sc, making a 9sc blk.

Continue to increase blks by 2sc on next 3 rounds. Check the diagram at each round.

Round 6 Work 5 x 9sc blks.

Round 7 Work 5 x 11sc blks.

Round 8 Work 5 x 13sc blks. This round ends with the 5th of the 13 sc blks.

It is here that the blks of sc begin to decrease and there are now ch-4 loops between the blks.

Round 9 *ch4, 1sc in next loop, ch4, skip 1sc, 1sc in each of the next 11sc, leave the last sc unworked, repeat from* 4 more times (5 x 11sc blks).

Round 10 *ch4, 1sc in next loop, ch4, 1sc in next loop, ch4, skip 1sc, 1sc in each next 9sc, repeat from* 4 more times.

Round 11 *(ch4, 1sc in next loop) 3 times, ch4, skip 1sc, 1sc in each next 7sc, repeat from* 4 more times.

Round 12 *(ch4, 1sc in next loop) 4 times, ch4, skip 1sc, 1sc in each next 5sc, repeat from* 4 more times.

Round 13 *(ch4, 1sc in next loop) 5 times, ch4, skip 1sc, 1sc in each next 3sc, repeat from* 4 more times. The spiral design is complete.

Round 14 ch4 (mark 4th ch with a safety pin, this ensures the correct placing of the sl st at the end of the round), 1sc in next loop, *(ch4, 1sc in next loop) 5 more times, ch4, skip 1sc, 1hdc in next sc, ch4, skip 1sc, 1sc in next loop, repeat from* 3 more times. End with ch4, 1sc in the next loop, 5 times, ch4, skip 1sc, 1hdc in next sc, ch4, sl st to the 4th of the ch-4 (marked) at the beginning of the round.

Round 15 Work firmly. ch1, 4sc in each of the next 2 loops, 5sc in next (corner) loop. Mark the center sc of the completed 5sc group. *4sc in the next 6 loops, 5sc in the next (corner) loop, mark the center sc as before, repeat from* 3 more times.

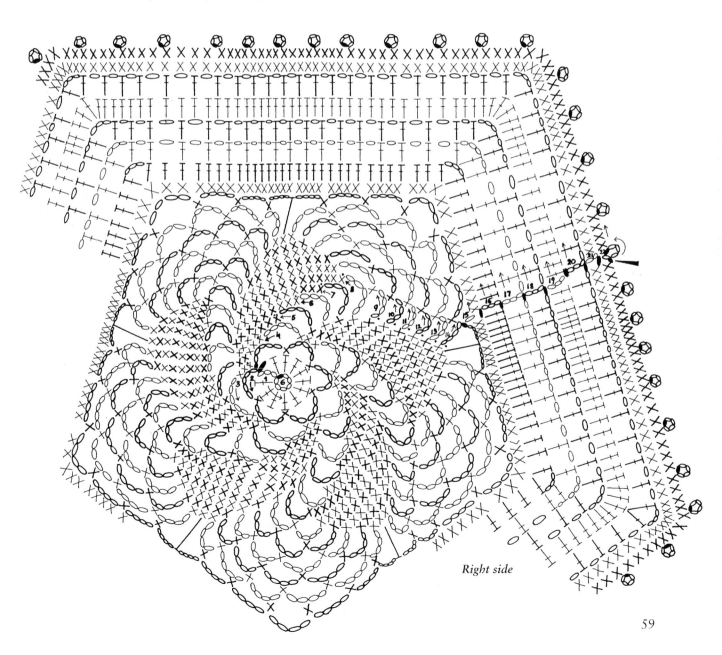

Right side

59

End with 4sc in the last 4 loops, sl st in the first sc at the beginning of this round.

Round 16 Work firmly. ch3 (to count as 1 dc), 1dc in each of the next 9sc, *work a corner group (1dc, ch3, 1dc) in the next corner sc (marked), 1dc in each of the next 28sc, repeat from* 3 more times. End with (1dc, ch3, 1dc) in the next corner sc, 1dc in remaining 18sts, sl st to the 3rd of the ch-3.

Round 17 ch4 (to count as 1dc and ch-1), skip st at the base of ch-4 and next dc, 1dc in next dc, *ch1, skip a dc, 1dc in next dc, repeat from* till 5sps made. Work ch1, (1dc, ch3, 1dc) in the next corner loop. *ch1, skip a dc, 1dc in next dc, repeat from* till 15 x ch-1 sps from corner loop, ch1, (1dc, ch3, 1dc) in corner loop. Continue round the remaining sides. End with ch1, skip a dc, sl st to the 3rd of ch-4 at the beginning of the round. **All 5 sides should have 16 x ch-1 sps between the corner loops.**

Round 18 ch4 (to count as 1dc and ch-1), skip ch1, 1dc in next dc, *ch1, skip 1ch, 1dc in next dc, repeat from* till 6sps made, ch1, (1dc, ch3, 1dc) in corner loop, *ch1, 1dc in next dc, repeat from* till 17 x ch-1 sps from corner loop, ch1, (1dc, ch3, 1dc) in corner loop. Continue round the remaining sides. End with ch1, sl st to the 3rd of the ch-4 at the beginning of the round. **All 5 sides should have 18 x ch-1 sps between the corner loops.**

Round 19 ch3 (to count as 1dc), *1dc in ch-1 sp, 1dc in dc, repeat from* on all 5 sides, working 5dc in the corner loops (see diagram). Mark center sc as before. End with 1dc in the last ch sp, sl st in the first dc (**not** the ch3).

Round 20 ch4 (to count as 1dc and ch-1), skip st at the base of the ch-4 and the next dc, 1dc in next dc, *ch1, skip 1dc, 1dc in next dc, repeat from* till 8sps made, ch3, 1dc in same st as last dc (1st corner loop). *ch1, skip a dc, 1dc in next dc, repeat from* till 21sps from corner loop, ch3, 1dc in the same st as last dc (2nd corner). Continue till the end of the round, following the diagram. End with ch1, sl st to the 3rd of the ch-4. **All 5 sides should have 21 x ch-1 sps between the corner loops. Adjust if necessary.**

Round 21 Work firmly. ch2 (to count as 1sc) *1sc in sp, 1sc in dc, repeat from* on all 5 sides, working 5sc in corner loops. End with a sl st in the 2nd of the ch-2.

For a neater finish, work this last round using a No 8 / 1.25 mm crochet hook.

Round 22 ch4, sl st to the first of ch-4 (1 x ch4 picot is completed) *1sc in each next 4sc, 1 x ch4 picot, repeat from* till the end of the round. End with a sl st to the base of the first picot.

It may be necessary to adjust the placing of the picots, so that they fall neatly at the corners of the work. Press lightly on the wrong side, using a damp cloth. Leave to dry.

Make up the pochette, using the pattern on page 17. Slip-stitch the crochet motif, or, as on the photographed example, use narrow embroidery ribbon and a tapestry needle to attach the lace to the bag (remember that you may need to remove it for washing). Tie the ends of the ribbon with a tiny bow. Attach a small Velcro dot to close the bag and add a pretty button.

BUTTERFLY & DAISY PANEL

Approximate size: 22 x 19 in

MATERIALS. 6 oz / 150 g white bedspread-weight cotton thread / No 10, a No 7 / 1.50 mm crochet hook, fabric to back the panel or to make up the cushion cover

STITCHES, ABBREVIATIONS & SYMBOLS

□ = 1sp

⊠ = 1blk

□⊠⊠□ = 1sp, 2blks, 1sp

TENSION / GAUGE

= 6sps

← 1 in →

WORKING NOTES
- ch1 between dcs on open mesh
- Mark every 50th ch st with a safety pin. This avoids having to recount from the start, if you lose count on this long chain.
- It may help to color each row as you work on a photocopy of the diagram.

BEGIN. ch222 (firmly). See diagram on pages 64-65.

Row 1   1dc in 6th ch from hook, *ch1, skip 1ch, 1dc in the next ch, continue from* to the end of the chain (109sps), ch4, turn.
If the first row of the work appears loose or wavy, use a smaller hook to work the ch and the first row.

Row 2   Skip 1ch, 1dc in next dc, *ch1, skip 1ch, 1dc in the next ch, continue from* ch4, turn.

Row 3   As row 2.

Row 4   Skip 1ch, 1dc in next dc, *ch1, skip 1ch, 1dc in next dc, repeat from* once more (until 3sps from start of row). 1dc in ch-1 sp, 1dc in dc, repeat from* till 3sps remain at the end of the previous row. ch1, skip 1ch, 1dc in next dc, ch1, skip 1ch, 1dc in dc, ch1, skip 1ch. End with 1dc in the 3rd of the ch-4 (3sps at the end of the row), ch4, turn.

From row 5   Continue to work blks and sps as shown on the graph diagram until all 109 rows are complete. **Do not finish off.**

PANEL EDGING
With the right side of the work facing you, work, 1sc in the first sp, *1sc in st, 1sc in sp, 1sc in st, 1 x ch5 picot. Repeat from*, working an extra 2sc in corners, till all 4 edges are complete. Finish off, weave in ends.

TO COMPLETE
Press the panel lightly on the wrong side, using a damp cloth. Ease into shape and, if necessary, pin out on a large board, covered with plastic wrap. Leave to dry. Make a backing for the filet panel, using a fabric of your choice. Put a channel at the back to enable you to slip in a hanging pole. The panel can also be mounted on a fabric-covered board. In both cases, use tiny slip stitches to attach the work to the backing. The panel can also be mounted on a pillowcase – see our example on page 66.

Left. Detail from the border. On page 66 you can see the panel mounted on a pillowcase.

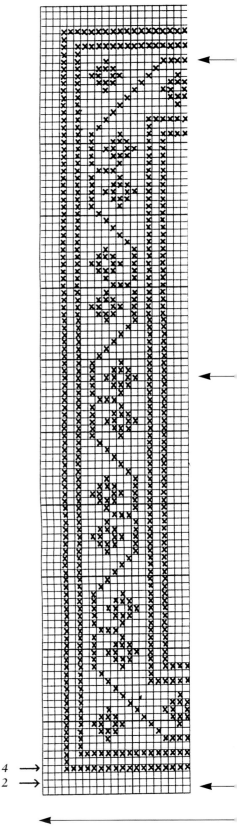

4 →
2 →

ch222 (109 spaces)

← 5
← 3
← 1

KEY FOB OR SCISSOR KEEPER

Approximate size: 1½ in square

MATERIALS. Remnants of dark red, green, or any other color bedspread-weight cotton thread / No 10, a No 7 / 1.50 mm crochet hook, scraps of fine fabric, batting or soft card

WORKING NOTE

◆ Work all chs and sts firmly, tightening each st as you work.

FRONT OF THE FOB (including rose motif, see diagram 1)

BEGIN. ch6, sl st to form a ring.
Round 1 ch5, *1dc in ring, ch2, repeat from*

6 more times. End with a sl st to the 3rd of ch-3 (8 x ch-2 sps made). Do **not** turn on this, or any of the following rounds.

Round 2 (1sc, 1hdc, 1dc, 1hdc, 1sc) in each ch-2 sp till 8 petals are made. End with a sl st to the first sc.

Round 3 Continue to work in the same direction and, in the back of the first petal, work *ch4, 1sc around and under the stem of the next dc on round 1 (see diagram 2). Repeat from* till the end of the round. End with a sl st to the first ch at the beginning of the round (8 loops made).

DIAGRAM 1 *Front of the fob*

The green scissor keeper is shown from the back.

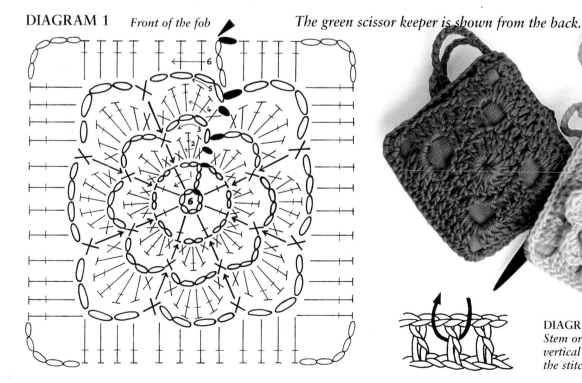

DIAGRAM 2
Stem or post (the vertical part of the stitch)

Round 4 (1sc, 1hdc, 3dc, 1hdc, 1sc) in each ch-4 loop, till 8 petals are made. End with a sl st to the first sc.

Round 5 Working behind the petals: *ch4, carefully work 1sc around the stem of the sc on round 3. Repeat from* till the end of the round. End with a sl st to the first of ch-4 (8 loops made).

Round 6 (ch3, 3dc) in the first loop, *(4dc, ch5, 4dc) in next loop, 4dc in the next loop, repeat from* 2 more times. End with (4dc, ch5, 4dc) in the last loop, sl st to 3rd of ch-3. Finish off, weave in ends.

BACK OF THE FOB (see diagram 3)

BEGIN. ch6, sl st to form a ring.

Round 1 ch3 (to count as 1dc), 15dc in ring (16 sts including ch-3), sl st to the 3rd of ch-3, ch3, turn.

Round 2 1dc in each of the next 3dc, *ch5, 1dc in each of the next 4dc, repeat from* 2 more times. End with ch5, sl st to the 3rd of ch-3, ch3, turn.

DIAGRAM 3

Back of the fob or scissor keeper

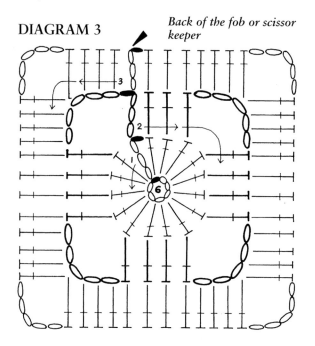

Round 3 (4dc, ch5, 4dc) in the corner loop, *1dc in each of the next 4dc, (4dc, ch5, 4dc) in the next corner loop, repeat from* 2 more times. End with 1dc in each of the remaining 3dc, sl st to the 3rd of ch-3. Finish off, weave in ends.

INNER PAD
Cut a square of thin batting slightly smaller than the crochet pouch. Cover in a fine material of your choice. The batting can be replaced by a square of card for a firmer and flatter finish to the fob.

TO COMPLETE
Press the front and the back of the work lightly, opening out the petals of the Irish rose and easing into 2 neat square shapes of equal size. With wrong sides together, and with the rose motif facing you, tie the thread once through the back and the front of any 2 corner loops, linking the 2 sections. Use a smaller hook to give a neat, firm edge to your work. Join the sections together by inserting the hook in the same corner loops and pulling the thread through to make a working loop.

Work ch2, 2sc in the same corner loops. Insert the hook carefully under the top 2 threads of the first dc on the rose motif and through the top 2 threads of the opposite dc on the back section, complete 1sc st. Continue to link the next 11dc along this first edge in the same way till you reach the next corner space, *5sc in the corner loop, link the next 12dc as before, repeat from* once more. Hold the loop with a safety pin. Insert the pad into the casing, remove the safety pin. Link the 2 edges of the remaining side together, as before. End with 2sc in the last corner loop, sl st to the 2nd of ch2.

Do **not** finish off. Work ch100, firmly, a sl st in the st at the base of the ch100, cut the thread, pass the tail end back through the working loop, pull tight to secure. Weave in ends.

PRETTY FANS FOR A GUEST TOWEL

Approximate size: each border measures 16 in (2 per towel). The length can be adjusted to fit the towel)

MATERIALS. 1 oz / 25 g écru bedspread-weight cotton thread / No 10, a No 7 / 1.50 mm crochet hook, a guest towel – approximately 25 x 16 in

SPECIAL STITCHES

 = *5 loop stitch (instructions on page 13)*

TENSION / GAUGE

One full 'fan' motif measures 2¼ in along the straight edge and one 'half fan' 1¼ in. Make a sample which includes both the full and the half fan. Measure it carefully to calculate the length of the border (see working notes below). Compare it with the width of the towel. If necessary, reduce or increase the size of the hook until you arrive at the correct length for the towel.

WORKING NOTES

◆ The border begins with one full fan and continues with half fans, hence multiples of half fans are required. A special edging is added once the length of fan motifs is complete.

◆ Work **all** chs and sts firmly and follow diagram throughout the work.

BEGIN. ch9, sl st to form a ring.

Row 1 ch2, 11hdc in ring, ch4, turn.

Note: This round should fill only half the ring, leaving the remaining ch to form the straight edge of the fan border.

Row 2 Skip st at the base of ch-4 and next st, 1dc in the next st, *ch1, 1dc in the next st, repeat from*. End with last dc in the 2tch on the row before (10 x ch-1 sps made), ch5, turn.

Row 3 *1 x 5 loop puff st in ch-1 sp, ch2, repeat from* till 10 puff sts made. End with ch2, 1dc in the 3rd of ch-4 on the row before, ch6, turn.

Row 4 1dc in st on top of puff st (under 2 threads), *ch3, skip 2ch, 1dc in st on top of next puff st, repeat from*. End with ch3, 1dc in 3rd of ch-5 (11 x ch-3 sps made), turn.

Row 5 Work *(1sc, 1hdc, 1dc, 1hdc, 1sc) in ch-3 sp (one shell made). Repeat from* in each ch-3 sp (11 shells) This completes one whole fan. Continue, adding half-fan motifs to

DIAGRAM 1 *(Right side)*

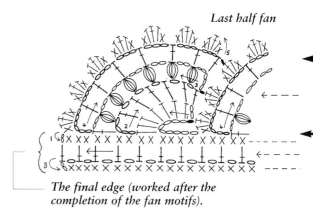

Last half fan

The final edge (worked after the completion of the fan motifs).

complete the required length, as follows:

FIRST HALF FAN
Work ch9, turn, sl st to the center dc of the first shell, ch2, turn.

Row 1 7hdc in the ch-9 loop, ch4, turn.

Row 2 Skip st at the base of the ch-4 and next st, *1dc in next st, ch1, repeat from* until 6 x ch-1 sps, omit last ch st, sl st to the center dc of the next shell, ch5, turn.

Row 3 1 x 5 loop puff st in the first ch-1 sp, *ch2, skip 1dc, 1 x 5 loop puff st in the next ch-1 sp, repeat from* till 6 puff sts are made. End with ch2, 1dc in the 3rd of ch-4, ch6, turn.

Row 4 1dc in st on top of puff st, *ch3, skip 2ch, 1dc in st on top of next puff st, repeat from*. End with ch3, 1dc in 3rd of ch-5 (7 x ch-3 sps made), sl st to center dc of the next shell, turn.

Row 5 (1sc, 1hdc, 1dc, 1hdc, 1sc) in each ch-3 sp (7 shells made). This completes 1 half fan. Check your tension once again and make sure it is the same as in the sample you worked at the beginning. Once the required number of repeats is complete, hold the working loop with a safety pin. Press lightly with a steam iron, easing the lace to the required length. Leave to dry.

FINAL EDGE
Turn border upside down in readiness to work along the straight edge.

Row 1 ch2, *1sc in sc, 2sc in each next 3sps, 2sc in the side of hdc, 4sc in next ch sp (13sc over the length of half fan, see diagram). Repeat from* over each **half fan**. Over last **full** fan, work 1sc in sc, 2sc in each of the next 3sps, 2sc in the side of hdc, 4sc in next sp, 2sc in the side of ch-2, 2sc in each of the next 3sps, 1sc in sc, ch4, turn.

Row 2 Skip st at base of ch-4, *1dc in next st, ch1, skip a st, repeat from* to the end. End with 1dc in last st. Adjust placing of last dc if necessary to complete the row, ch2, turn.

Row 3 *1sc in ch-1 sp, 1sc in dc, repeat from* to the end. End with 1sc in last sp and 1sc in the 3rd of 4tch. Finish off, weave in ends. Make an identical border for the other end of the towel.

TO COMPLETE
Press the 2 lengths of lace lightly, using a steam iron. Pin out on a board covered with plastic wrap, easing the lace to the length required and leave to dry. Pin the borders carefully along each end of the guest towel: the lace should overlap slightly over the edge of the towel. Ease to fit. Slip-stitch into place.

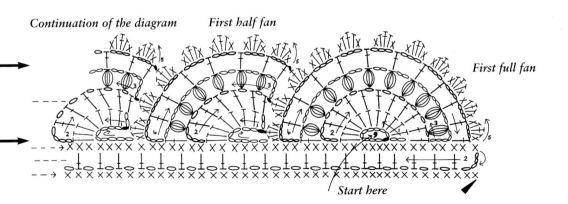

Continuation of the diagram   *First half fan*

First full fan

Start here

This guest towel will make a lovely present for someone, or give a touch of bygone elegance to a romantic bathroom.

BREAD BASKET LINER

Approximate size of open liner: 16 in square

MATERIALS. 4 oz / 100 g green bedspread-weight cotton thread / No 10, a No 7 / 1.50 mm crochet hook, a bread basket about 12 in square

STITCHES, ABBREVIATIONS & SYMBOLS

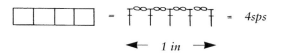

☐ = ⌐¯¯⌐ = *1sp*   ☒ = ⫟⫟⫟⫟ = *1blk*

☐☒☒☐ = ⌐¯⫟⫟⫟⫟⫟⫟¯⌐ = *1sp, 2blks, 1sp*

TENSION / GAUGE

☐☐☐☐☐ = ⌐¯⌐¯⌐¯⌐¯⌐ = *4sps*

← *1 in* →

WORKING NOTES

♦ ch2 between dcs on open mesh
♦ The square center section of the liner is worked first, then the 4 triangular flaps.
♦ In the center square section, all rounds start with ch5, except for round 2. All rounds finish with ch2 and 1dc in center ch of ch-5, except for round 2. All rounds are worked in the same direction within the center square.
♦ Keep the tension firm and even and follow the stitch diagram as you work.

CENTER SQUARE (see diagram 1 on page 74)

BEGIN ch6, sl st to form a ring.

Round 1 ch5 (to count as 1dc and ch-2), 1dc in the ring, *ch5, 1dc in the ring, ch2, 1dc in the ring, repeat from* 2 more times. End with ch2, 1dc in the 3rd of ch-5 (8sps forming a square). **Do not turn.**

Round 2 ch3, 2dc in sp, 1dc in the same ch as the last dc on round 1, 2dc in next sp, 1dc in dc, *(3dc, ch5, 3dc) in ch-5 sp, 1dc in dc, 2dc in the next sp, 1dc in dc, repeat from* 2 more times. End with 2dc in ch-2 sp, 1dc in dc, ch2, 1dc in the 3rd of ch-3. **Do not turn.**

Round 3 ch5, 1dc in the same ch as the last dc (the space just formed is the start of round 3). Mark this first space with a safety pin. Remove and replace this marker as you start each of the next 19 rounds. The space count will not match the other 3 sides till the last space on the round is complete. *ch2, skip 2dc, 1dc in each next 4dc, ch2, skip 2dc, 1dc in next dc, ch2, skip 2ch (1dc, ch5, 1dc) in the center ch of ch-5, ch2, skip 2ch, 1dc in dc, repeat from* 2 more times, ch2, skip 2dc, 1dc in each of the next 4dc, ch2, skip 2dc, 1dc in next dc, ch2, skip 2ch, 1dc in next dc. End with ch2, skip 2ch, 1dc in the center ch of ch-5 (hook under 2 threads if possible).

Note: The side facing you is the right side of the work, mark the **wrong** side with a contrast thread for future reference.

Round 4 ch5, 1dc in same ch as last dc (remove and replace the safety pin in the new ch-5 sp as before). *ch2, skip 2ch, 1dc in next dc.

Continue working a round of open meshes. End with ch2, 1dc in the center ch of ch-5, at the beginning of the round.

Round 5 As round 4.

Round 6 Start of the ivy leaf design. Work all dc blks and chs firmly and evenly to keep the work flat. **Note:** Several blocks together are difficult to define, especially blocks over blocks, try multiplying the number of blocks on the graph by 3 and adding 1. Remember to count the first dc. Continue with round 6 as follows: ch5, 1dc in same st as last dc (mark this new space as before), ch2, skip 2ch, 1dc in next dc, *2dc in sp, 1dc in next dc, repeat from* 4 more times (5blks made). This is the start of the first ivy leaf.

Continue around the remaining 3 sides, as shown in diagram 1, ensuring that the first row of each ivy leaf is correctly positioned. End with ch2, 1dc in the center ch of ch-5.

Round 7 to round 22 see diagram 2.

Note: Every few rounds, make sure that the work lies flat. If satisfactory, press lightly with a steam iron and ease into shape. Allow to dry on a flat surface, then continue. If the work is not flat, continuing will make the problem worse. Unpick and start again, tightening up all chs and sts as you work: maintaining a firm and even tension throughout the work is essential. The last row of the center square should have 45 sps. **Do not finish off.** Hold the loop with a safety pin.

FOLD-OVER FLAPS (Diagram 3 shows in detail the beginning and the end of the rows.)

WORKING NOTES

◆ The flaps are added to the center square individually, so follow the diagram with

DIAGRAM 1 *(Right side) Stitch detail of the center square, showing the start and finish of each round.*

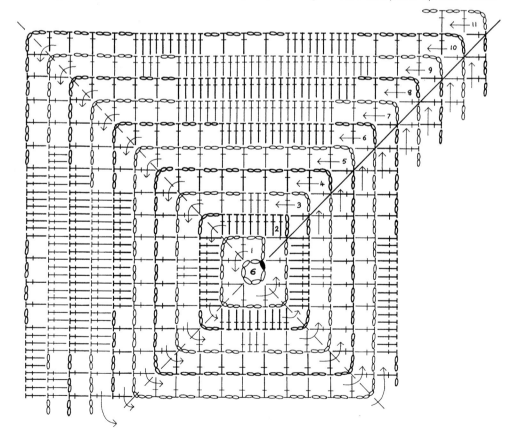

extra care as you change direction on each row.

- The ivy leaf design is reversed on the flaps.
- Work straight for the first 8 rows, then begin to decrease at the beginning and the end of each row, finishing with 1 block at the point of the flap.

- Work all turning chains firmly.
- It may be helpful to color each row on a photocopy of the diagram as you work.

FIRST FLAP

With right side facing, remove the safety pin and insert the hook in the working loop.

DIAGRAM 2
(Right side)

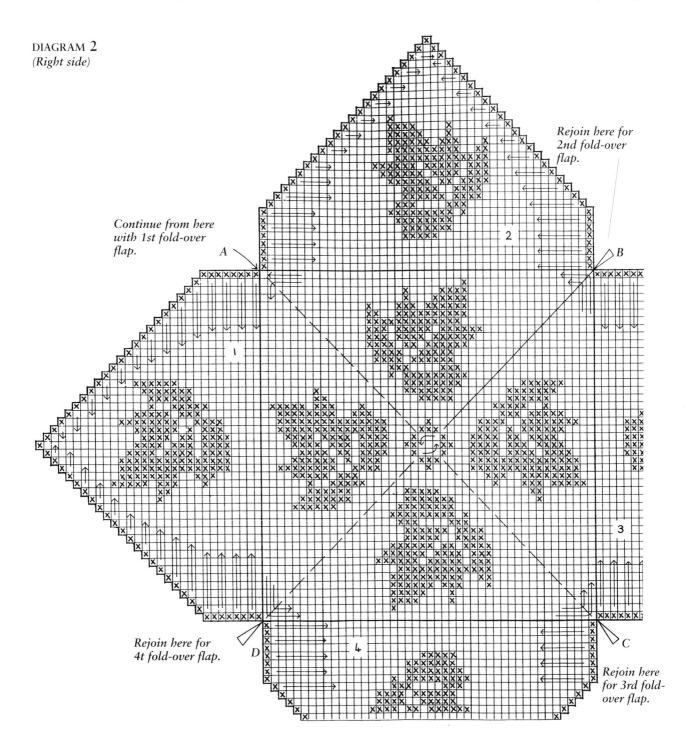

Continue from here with 1st fold-over flap.

Rejoin here for 2nd fold-over flap.

Rejoin here for 4t fold-over flap.

Rejoin here for 3rd fold-over flap.

Continue from point **A** on diagram 2. For stitch detail, see diagram 3.

Row 1   ch3 (to count as 1dc), 2dc in ch-2 sp, 1dc in next dc, *ch2, skip 2ch, 1dc in next dc, repeat from* to the last space but one. End with 3dc in the last sp, ch3, turn.

Row 2   1dc in each 3dc, *ch2, skip 2ch, 1dc in next dc, repeat from* to the end of the row. End with 1dc in each of the last 3dc and 1dc in 3tch, ch3, turn.

Row 3 and row 4   As row 2, turn.

Row 5   Start of the ivy leaf design. Work dc blks extra firmly. 1dc in each of next 3dc, *ch2, skip 2ch, 1dc in next dc, repeat from* till 20 sps are made, *2dc in ch-2 sp, 1dc in next dc, repeat from* till 5 blks are made. *ch2, skip 2ch, 1dc in next dc, repeat from* till 18 sps are made. End with 1dc in each of the last 3dc and 1dc in 3tch, ch3, turn.

Row 6, row 7 and row 8   As shown on diagram 3, omit ch3 at the end of row 8, turn.

Row 9   First row of decreases (see diagram 3). Skip first dc, sl st in each of the next 3dc, ch3, 2dc in ch-2 sp, 1dc in next dc, *ch2, skip 2ch, 1dc in next dc, repeat from*, working blks and sps as shown on diagram 3. End with 2dc in the last sp, 1dc in next dc, turn.

Row 10 to row 29   Still following diagram 2, decrease at the beginning and the end of each row, as on row 9, turn.

Row 30   Skip first dc, sl st in each of the next 3dc, ch3, 2dc in ch-2 sp, 1dc in dc. finish off. **Turn the work over** till the right side faces you. Continue with the 2nd flap.

SECOND FLAP
Join the thread by tying it once in the corner space **B**, follow instructions for 'flap 2' on diagram 2, starting from row 1.

THIRD FLAP
Join the thread to the corner space **C**, follow instructions for 'flap 2', as from row 1.

FOURTH FLAP

DIAGRAM **3**   *(Right side) Note that the ivy leaf design is reversed on the flaps (see also diagram 2). The diagram below shows the stitch detail of the beginning and the end of each row and the start of the decreases on the flaps.*

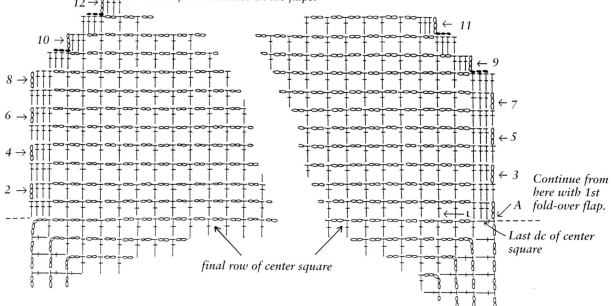

final row of center square

Continue from here with 1st fold-over flap.

Last dc of center square

Join the thread to the corner space **D**, follow instructions for 'flap 2', as from row 1.

TO COMPLETE
Weave in all tail ends. Press lightly with a steam iron, using a damp cloth. Ease into shape, pin out on a large board covered in plastic wrap. Leave to dry. Attach a chain and tassel to each end of the flaps. See page 26 for instructions.

This smaller version of the bread basket liner was produced using 4 oz / 100 g of bedspread-weight cotton thread / No 20 and a No 8 / 1.25 mm crochet hook.

ROSE NAPKIN RINGS

Approximate size: 2 in in diameter

MATERIALS. 2 oz / 50 g écru bedspread-weight cotton thread / No 10 – make 6 napkin rings, a No 7 / 1.50 mm crochet hook

TENSION / GAUGE

Check: the length of the 1st row, excluding the picot edge, should be 2½ in long.

WORKING NOTES

◆   Keep tension extra firm and even throughout.

BEGIN. ch29 firmly (see diagram 1).

Row 1   (1dc, ch3, 1dc) in the 6th ch from hook, *skip 3ch (1dc, ch3, 1dc) in the next ch st. Repeat from* 4 more times, skip 2ch, 1dc in the last ch st, ch2, turn. See tension / gauge check above.

DIAGRAM 1 *(Right side)*

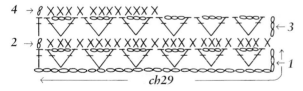

ch29

DIAGRAM 2 *(Wrong side)*
Detail of the last row and start of the finished edge with the picots in place

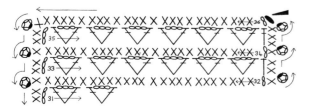

Row 2   3sc in ch-3 sp, *1sc in sp between 2dc, 3sc in ch-3 sp, repeat from* 4 more times. End with 1sc in the last sp, ch3, turn.

Row 3   Skip st at the base of ch-3 and next st, *(1dc, ch3, 1dc) in next st, skip 3sts, repeat from* 5 more times. End with 1dc in the 2nd of ch-2, ch2, turn. Rows 2 and 3 form the lace pattern.

Repeat rows 2 and 3 till 36 rows are complete, omitting the ch-3 at the end of the last row. Do not finish off. Mark the side of the work facing you with a contrast thread – this is the **wrong** side of the work.

PICOT EDGING (see diagram 2)
(The picot is worked on the 2 long sides only.) With the wrong side still facing you, turn the work and begin to work along the first long edge of the napkin ring. (1sc, 1 x ch4 picot, 2sc) in same sp as last sc, 1sc in the side of sc (row end), 1 x ch4 picot, *2sc in next sp, 1sc in the side of next sc, 1 x ch4 picot, repeat from* till you reach the next corner sp, 4sc in corner sp.

Note: If the edging is loose or wavy, try using a smaller hook.

Start along the first short side (no picots on short sides): *1sc between 2dc, 3sc in ch-3 sp, repeat from* till the next corner, 4sc in the corner sp. Work along the other long side as follows: *1sc in the side of ch-2 (row end), (1 x ch4 picot, 2sc) in next sp, repeat from* to the end of the long side. End with (3sc, 1 x ch4 picot) in the last sp, sl st to ch-2 at the beginning of the short side. Keep a long tail end for stitching the seam. Finish off and weave in the short tail end to the wrong side of the work. Press the finished strip lightly on the wrong side before continuing. Do **not** sew the seam and make into a ring at this stage. The Irish rose motif must be worked first.

IRISH ROSE MOTIF (see diagram 3)

BEGIN. ch6, sl st to form a ring.

Round 1 ch6 (to count as 1dc and ch-3), 1dc in ring, *ch3, 1dc in ring, repeat from* till 5sps are made. End with ch3, sl st to the 3rd of ch-3 (6 spaces made). Do not turn.

Round 2 (1sc, 1hdc, 3dc, 1hdc, 1sc) in each ch-3 loop till round, sl st to first sc (6 petals). Do not turn.

Round 3 Continue working in the same direction and, in the back, behind the first petal, work: *ch5, 1sc around and under the stem or post of the next dc on round 1 (see diagram 4), ch5, repeat from* till round. End with a sl st to first ch at the beginning of the round (6 loops made). Do not turn.

Round 4 (1sc, 1hdc, 5dc, 1hdc, 1sc) in each ch-5 loop till round. End with a sl st to first sc. Do not turn.

Round 5 Working in the back, behind the 1st petal, *ch5, work a sc around and under sc on round 3 (make sure you position this st accurately), ch5, repeat from* till round. End with a sl st to first of ch-5 (6 loops made). Do not turn.

Round 6 (1sc, 1hdc, 6dc, 1hdc, 1sc) in each ch-5 loop till round. End with a sl st to the first sc. Finish off, weave in ends. The Irish rose motif is now complete.

MAKING UP THE NAPKIN RING

Pin the rose motif in the center of the strip and on the right side of the work. Use matching sewing thread to attach the rose neatly into place. Stitch the side seam of the ring, working from the wrong side of the work and using the long tail end of thread. Turn the work so that the rose faces you and gently pull the petals into shape. Touch up with a steam iron, if necessary.

DIAGRAM 3
(Right side)

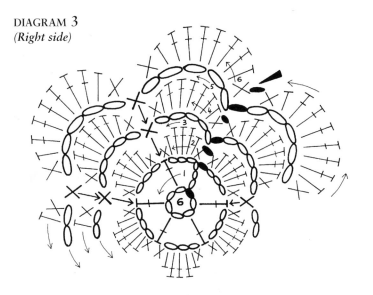

DIAGRAM 4
Stem or post (the vertical part of the stitch)

WALL HANGING

Approximate size of crochet panel: 30 x 5 in

MATERIALS. 3 oz / 75 g dark red bedspread-weight cotton thread/ No 10, a No 7 / 1.50 mm crochet hook, suitable fabric for mounting the hanging

STITCHES, ABBREVIATIONS & SYMBOLS

TENSION / GAUGE

WORKING NOTES
◆ ch1 between dcs on open mesh.
◆ Refer to graph diagram as you work and keep the tension firm and even.

BEGIN. ch56 (see diagram 1 on page 83).

Row 1 1dc in 6th ch from hook, *ch1, skip 1ch, 1dc in next ch, repeat from* to the end of the row (26sps), ch4, turn.

Row 2 Skip 1ch, 1dc in next dc, *ch1, skip 1ch, 1dc in next dc, repeat from*. At the end, skip 1ch, 1dc in next ch, ch4, turn.

Row 3 to row 7 As row 2.

Row 8 Skip 1ch, 1dc in next dc, *ch1, skip 1ch, 1dc in next dc, repeat from* till 7sps, 1dc in next sp, 1dc in next dc (one blk made), *ch1,

skip 1ch, 1dc in next dc, repeat from* to the end of the row (18sps), ch4, turn. Continue, following diagram 1 and working blks and sps till the grapevine design is complete. Work 7 more rows of basic filet crochet mesh as explained in row 2, omitting the last ch4 on the final row (153 rows). Do not cut the thread. Hold the loop with a safety pin. Before continuing, press the work lightly on the wrong side, using a damp cloth.

EDGING
Remove the safety pin. With right side facing, work along the first **long side** of the crochet panel (see diagram 2 for stitch detail). Tighten each sc as you work the st.

BEGIN. ch2, 2sc in corner sp, 2sc in each sp along the left-hand side of the panel, 5sc in the corner sp. Work along the lower edge of the panel as follows: *1sc in next dc, 1sc in sp, repeat from* to the next corner sp, 5sc in the corner sp, 2sc in each sp along the right hand side of the panel, 5sc in the corner sp. Work along the top edge as follows: *1sc in next dc, 1sc in sp, repeat from* to the last corner sp, sl st to the 2nd of ch-2 at the start of edging, turn.

Change to a hook one size smaller for the final round. Work firmly as follows: *ch3, skip a st, 1sc in next st, repeat from* on all 4 sides. This last round should lie flat. End with a sl st to the base of the ch-3 at the beginning of the round. Finish off, weave in ends to the wrong side of the panel.

The panel can be mounted on a piece of fabric, as illustrated on page 84, or framed (avoid glass).

DIAGRAM 1
(Right side)

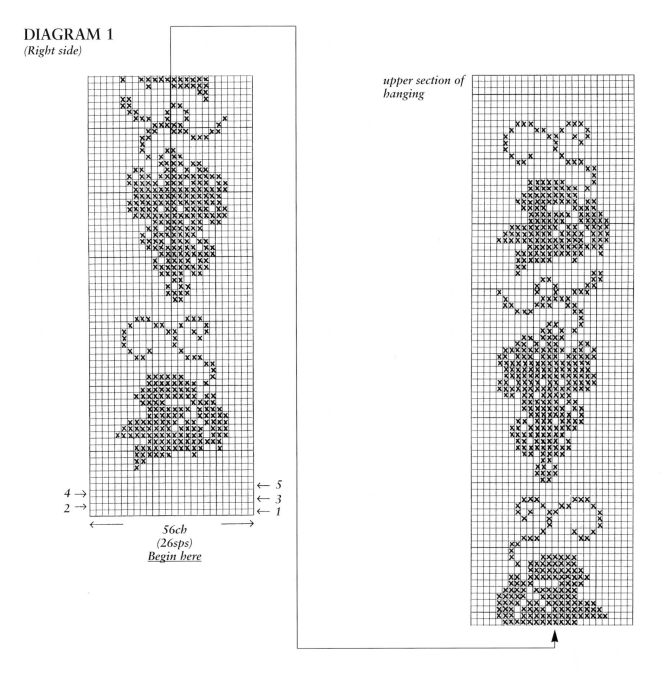

upper section of hanging

4 → 2 →

← 5
← 3
← 1

56ch
(26sps)
Begin here

DIAGRAM 2 *(Right side) Stitch detail of the start and finish of the edging*

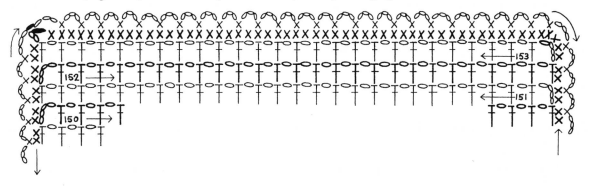

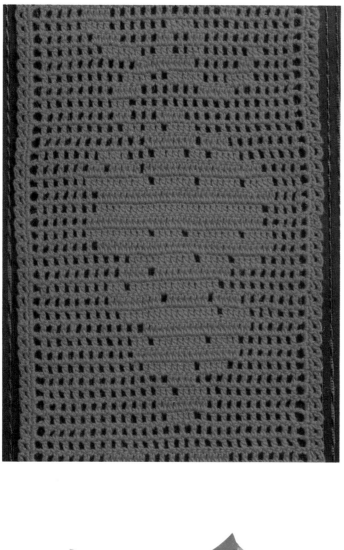

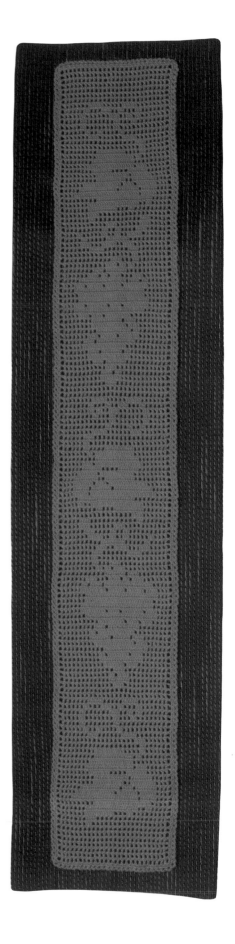

TISSUE BOX COVER

Approximate size: 9 x 4⅛ x 2¾ in. The size of the boxes may vary slightly according to the brand. By adjusting the tension, the pattern can be made to fit most rectangular boxes, containing 150 tissues.

MATERIALS. 3 oz / 75 g white bedspread-weight cotton/ No 10 (the quantity given allows for slight variations in box sizes), a No 7 / 1.50 mm crochet hook, 1 standard box of 150 tissues

STITCHES, ABBREVIATIONS & SYMBOLS

TENSION / GAUGE

WORKING NOTES

◆ ch1 between dcs on open mesh
◆ It is advisable to make a sample to check

the tension: ch26, work a basic mesh over 5 or 6 rows. If necessary, change the hook size to achieve the correct number of spaces over a given measurement. (The tension given applies to the box measurements above.)

◆ Follow the diagrams carefully and keep the tension firm and even throughout.
◆ An odd number of spaces is required for the butterfly and the bow designs on the sides of the box.
◆ To improve the shape of the last space at the end of each row, try skipping 2ch instead of 1ch, the last dc in the next ch st and working always under 2 threads.

STAGE ONE – TOP PANELS OF THE BOX

Follow diagram 1 – you will see that the top of the box is formed by 2 panels, bearing the butterfly design.

BEGIN

First panel: ch106, worked fairly tight.

Row 1   1dc in the 6th ch from hook, *ch1, skip

DIAGRAM 1   *(Right side) The panels which will form the top of the box*

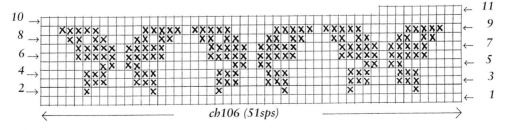

ch106 (51sps)

ch1, 1dc in next ch, repeat from* to the end of the row (51sps), ch4, turn. At this stage check that the tension is correct and that your first row measures **exactly** the same as the top of the box. If this first row is too long or loose, try using a smaller hook; if too short and tight, use a hook one size bigger. **It is vital** to ensure that this first row is the correct length and has the required number of spaces, or you may discover at the end of all your efforts that the finished cover does not fit!

Row 2 Skip 1ch, 1dc in the next dc, *ch1, skip 1ch, 1dc in the next ch, repeat from* till 5sps from beginning of row, 1dc in next sp, 1dc in dc (1blk made), the first block of the butterfly design. Continue along this row, following the butterfly design on diagram 1. At the end of the row, skip 1ch, 1dc in next ch, ch4, turn.

Row 3 to row 9 will complete the butterfly design.

Row 10 Work 1 more row of filet crochet mesh, beyond the butterfly design. These 10 rows should be 2 in deep.

Row 11 Work a **short** row as follows: skip 1ch, 1dc in next dc, *ch1, skip 1ch, 1dc in the next ch, repeat from* till 10sps from the beginning of the row. Leave a long tail end and finish off.

SECOND PANEL
Work exactly as the first.

Press both panels lightly, using a damp cloth. Before sewing together, check that both panels, when placed together as in diagram 2, fit the top of the box **exactly**. Ensure that the short 10sp rows are placed towards the center of the box. This will form the opening to pull out the tissues.

Using the cotton tail, stitch the short 10sp row on panel 1 to the opposite 10sps on panel 2, matching dc to dc and sp to sp. A neat seam can be achieved if you take the needle under the top 2 threads of the dcs as you sew them together. Do **not** sew too tightly. Repeat with the other 10sp section. Weave in all tail ends. For future reference mark the wrong side of the completed panels with a contrasting thread. Press lightly with a steam iron on the wrong side, using a damp cloth. Ease to fit the top of the box.

STAGE TWO – SIDE PANELS
(See diagram 4 on page 88 for the bow design.)

WORKING NOTES
- The 4 sides of the cover are worked in one continuous section and the bows are worked starting from the top of the design.
- On round 1 work to a firmer tension by tightening each sc as you complete the st, especially on the long sides
- Also on round 1, it is important to mark the center sc of the 5sc, at each corner, with a safety pin

BEGIN. With right side facing (see diagram 3), tie the thread into the top left-hand corner, as shown.

DIAGRAM 2 *Position of the 2 top panels, ready for assembly*

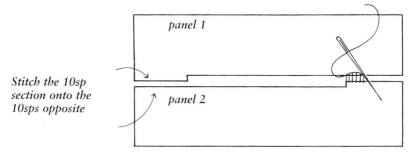

Stitch the 10sp section onto the 10sps opposite

panel 1

panel 2

Round 1   Short side. Work firmly, ch1, 5sc beside ch1 in the first corner sp, **mark the center sc** under the top 2 threads, *2sc in each next 10sps, **work 1sc on sewn seam**, 2sc in the remaining 9sps, 5sc in corner sp, **mark center sc** (43sts between marked corner sts on short side). **Long side. 1sc in first sp**, 2sc in each remaining sp till you reach the next corner sp, 5sc in the next corner sp, **mark center sc** (101sts between the marked corner sts on the long side). Repeat from* on remaining 2 sides, remember: 1sc on sewn seam and **1sc only** in first sp on long side. Match st numbers between marked sts on opposite sides. Omit the 5sc in the last corner sp. End with a sl st to first sc of the corner group. Sl st **again** in each next 2 sc, remove the marker, ch4, turn.

Round 2   Long side. Start of the filet crochet mesh. Wrong side facing, skip st at the base of

ch-4 and next st, 1dc in the next st, *ch1, skip 1sc, 1dc in the next sc, repeat from* till you reach the marked st at the next corner. Remove marker. Work ch1, skip 1sc, (1dc, ch1, 1dc) in the corner st, replace marker in the newly formed corner sp (51sps excluding the corner sp). **Short side.** *ch1, skip 1sc, 1dc in next st, repeat from* till you reach the marked st at the next corner. Remove the marker, work ch1, skip 1sc, (1dc, ch1, 1dc) in the corner st, replace the marker in the newly formed corner sp (22sps, excluding the corner sps). Continue round the remaining 2 sides, marking the **new** corner sp. End with ch1, skip 1sc, 1dc at the base of ch-4 at the beginning of the round, ch1, sl st to 3rd of ch-4. This last sp forms a corner sp – mark this as before, ch4, turn. Your work will now begin to turn down on all 4 sides.

Round 3   Short side. Right side facing, skip

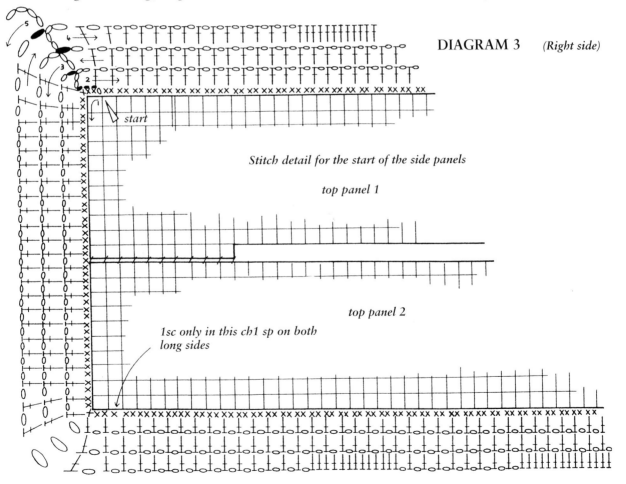

DIAGRAM 3   *(Right side)*

start

Stitch detail for the start of the side panels

top panel 1

top panel 2

1sc only in this ch1 sp on both long sides

1ch, 1dc in **next dc**, **mark** new corner sp, *ch1, skip 1ch, 1dc in the next dc, repeat from* till 22sps from the corner. Remove the marker, work ch1, skip 1ch, 1dc in the next dc, **mark** the new corner sp, *ch1, skip 1ch, 1dc in next dc, repeat from* till 51 sps from the corner, remove the marker, ch1, skip ch1, 1dc in next dc, **mark** the new corner sp. Continue round the last 2 sides, marking the new corner sp as before. End with ch1, sl st to the 3rd of ch-4, ch4, turn.

Note: The next round is the start of the bow design, which appears on the long sides only and is worked from the top of the cover down. You may find it easier to follow if you photocopy diagram 4 and turn it upside down. The short sides of the cover are worked in basic mesh.

Round 4   Long side. Wrong side facing, skip ch1, 1dc in next dc, *ch1, skip 1ch, 1dc in next dc, repeat from* till 15sps made, *1dc in the next sp, 1dc in dc, repeat from* till 6blks are made (start of bow design). Continue to work blks and sps according to diagram 4, working the 4 sides as one complete round. End each round with a sl st to the 3rd of ch-4, ch4, turn. Continue to mark the corners as a useful guide, turning the work after each round.

Round 5 to round 12   complete the bow design. End each round with a sl st to the 3rd of ch-4, ch4, turn.

Round 13   Skip 1ch, 1dc in next dc, *ch1, skip

1ch, 1dc in next dc, repeat from* till round all 4 sides. End with a sl st to the 3rd of ch-4, ch4, turn. Hold the loop with a safety pin.

At this stage, try the cover on the box, ease to fit neatly at the corners. The cover should almost reach the bottom edge of the box, leaving approximately ¼ in, ie. just enough space to add the final picot edge. Remove the safety pin and continue. **If the side panels are too short,** repeat round 13 once more or till the required depth is achieved. Then add the final picot edge as follows. Change to a smaller hook for a neater finish, work this last round with the **wrong** side of the work facing you to emphasize the picot.

PICOT EDGING
ch4, sl st to the first of ch-4, pull tight (1 x ch4 picot made), 1sc in ch-1 sp, 1sc in next dc, 1sc in next ch-1 sp, 1sc in next dc, repeat from till round all 4 sides. End with a sl st to the base of the first picot. Finish off.

THE EDGE TO THE CENTRAL OPENING
With right side facing, tie the thread to a ch-1 sp at the right-hand side of the opening. Work ch1, 2sc in each sp all round the opening. Sl st to the first sc at the beginning of the round. Finish off, weave in all tail ends.

TO COMPLETE
Press the sides of the cover lightly, using a damp cloth, taking care not to stretch the cover. Make a silk lining to go under the cover, see instructions on page 16.

DIAGRAM 4 (Right side) – Long side panels

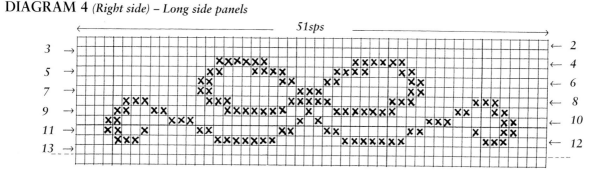

MAGNOLIA TABLECLOTH

Approximate size of the tablecloth: 39 in square (including chevron border). Each motif measures 6 in square and the border is 3 in deep.

MATERIALS. 16 oz / 450 g white bedspread-weight cotton thread No 10 – to make the tablecloth shown on page 95, which is composed of 36 motifs, and its border (4 oz / 100g will yield at least 9 motifs), a No 7 / 1.50 mm crochet hook, a box of small safety pins

SPECIAL STITCHES

 = work sc around and under post or stem of stitch

✕ = work sc in back single thread only

⊤ = work dc in back single thread only

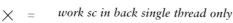 = single picot group

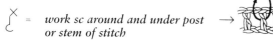 = double picot group

= open trc 'shell'

WORKING NOTES

◆ The final size of the work depends on the number of motifs. Multiply the size of a single motif, adding the width of the border, to decide how many you will need to produce the tablecloth or bedspread of your choice.
◆ Always work under the top 2 threads of all stitches unless otherwise stated.
◆ Work all stitches and chains firmly and follow the diagram opposite as you work.

◆ Use safety pins to mark stitches, as indicated in the text, to ensure accurate placing of stitches.

BEGIN. ch10, sl st to form a ring.

Round 1 ch1, 12sc in ring, sl st to first sc. Do not turn.

The petals are worked individually – follow diagram 1 very carefully.

Round 2 **First petal:** ch14, 1sc in the 3rd ch from hook, 1hdc in next ch, 1dc in each next 2ch, 1trc in each next 5ch, 1dc in each next 2ch, 1hdc in last ch, sl st to first sc on round 1, ch1, turn so that the wrong side of the work faces you, 1sc around/under the stem of each next 6sts, ch8 (start of the second petal).

Second petal: *1sc in 3rd ch from hook, 1hdc in next ch, 1dc in each next 2ch, 1trc in each next 2ch. Turn the work over till right side facing and continue along the remainder of the second petal: 1trc in each next 3sc, 1dc in each next 2sc, 1hdc in last sc, sl st to the next sc on round 1, ch1, turn the work so that the wrong side faces you, 1sc around/under stem of each next 6sts, ch8 (start of the next petal).

Work the other 10 petals as from* of the **second** petal, but **omitting** ch8 after the 6sc on the final petal. Leave a long tail end and finish off. Turn work to the wrong side, use the tail end to sew the 6sc on the **last** petal to the 6sts on the **first** petal, matching each stitch with the stitch opposite. Sew from the middle of the petals towards the center of the flower. This should leave a ridge on the right side to match the other petals. Sew the tail ends to the wrong side. Steam press very lightly on the wrong side to straighten out the petals.

Round 3   Right side facing. Insert the hook under 2 threads at the point of any of the petals, draw the cotton tail through and tie once. Insert the hook in the same place and draw through a working loop, ch1, 1sc beside ch1, *ch8 (tight), 1sc in the next petal point, ch8, 1sc in the next petal point, ch1, **turn**, (4sc, ch4, 4sc) in ch-8 loop, 1sc in sc, ch2, **turn**, **1trc in ch-4 loop, ch2, repeat from** 6 more times, skip 4sc, sl st in the next st (8 x ch-2 sps made = open trc 'shell'), ch8, 1sc in the next petal point, repeat from* till the end of the round. End with a sl st to the first sc at the beginning of the round.

Round 4   ch8 (to count as 1dc and ch-5), *skip 8ch, 1trc in st on the next petal point, see diagram 1. ch5, skip (2ch, 1trc, 2ch), 1dc in the next trc, ch5, skip (2ch, 1trc, 2ch). Work (1dc, ch5, 1dc) in next trc (corner group made), ch5, skip (2ch, 1trc, 2ch), 1dc in next trc, ch5, skip (2ch, 1trc, 2ch), 1trc in st on the next petal point, ch5, skip 8ch, 1dc in st on next petal point, ch5. Repeat from* 3 more times. Omit the final dc and ch5 on the last repeat. End with a sl st to the 3rd of ch-8 at the beginning of the round.

Round 5   ch4, skip st at the base of ch-4, 1dc in next ch, ch1, skip 1ch, 1dc in next ch, ch1, skip 1ch, 1dc in trc, *ch1, skip 1ch, 1dc in next ch, ch1, skip 1ch, 1dc in next ch, ch1, skip 1ch, 1dc in next dc, repeat from* once more. Work the corner group as follows: ch1, skip 1ch, 1dc in next ch, ch1, 1dc in the **next** ch, **mark** this corner with a safety pin (under 2 threads), ch1, 1dc in the **next** ch, ch1, **skip** 1ch, 1dc in next dc,

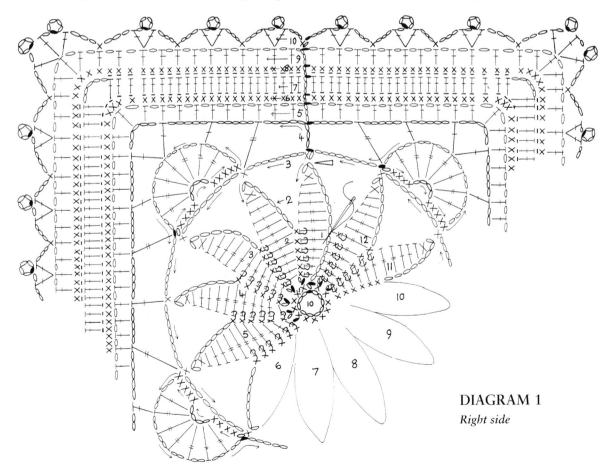

DIAGRAM 1
Right side

(the corner group is complete). Continue round the remaining sides, working ch-1 sps and corner groups as before. Mark the center dc of the corner groups for future reference. End with ch1, skip 1ch, sl st to the 3rd of ch-4 at the beginning of the round (22 x ch-1 sps between the marked corners).

Note: Work all sts on rounds 6, 7, and 8 extra firmly.

Round 6   ch2, *1sc in sp, 1sc in dc, repeat from* till you reach the marked corner st, remove the marker, work 3sc in that st, replace the marker in the center sc (under 2 threads). Continue to work from first* along the remaining sides. End with a sl st to ch-2 at the beginning of the round.

Round 7   ch3 (to count as 1dc), 1dc in each st, working into the **back single thread only**, till you reach the marked st, remove the marker,

work (1dc, ch5, 1dc) in that corner st. Continue round the remaining sides, working 1dc in each st and working (1dc, ch5, 1dc) in the marked corner sts. End with a sl st to the 3rd of ch-3. **Note:** There should be 47dcs between the corner sps on each side. Adjust the number of sts, if and when necessary – it is important to have the correct stitch count on each side.

Round 8   ch2, *1sc in each st, work into the **back single thread only**, till you reach the corner ch-5 sp, 5sc in corner sp, **mark** the center sc of 5sc, repeat from*, till the remaining sides are complete.

Note: take care **not** to skip the first dc after 5sc in the corner. End with a sl st to ch-2.

Round 9   ch4, skip st at the base of ch-4 and next st, 1dc in the next st (under **2** threads), *ch1, skip a st, 1dc in the next st, repeat from*

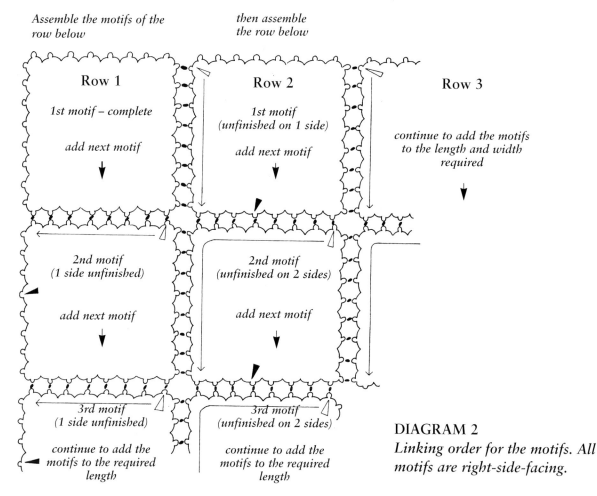

Assemble the motifs of the row below

then assemble the row below

Row 1

1st motif – complete

add next motif

Row 2

1st motif (unfinished on 1 side)

add next motif

Row 3

continue to add the motifs to the length and width required

2nd motif (1 side unfinished)

add next motif

2nd motif (unfinished on 2 sides)

add next motif

3rd motif (1 side unfinished)

continue to add the motifs to the required length

3rd motif (unfinished on 2 sides)

continue to add the motifs to the required length

DIAGRAM 2
Linking order for the motifs. All motifs are right-side-facing.

till 12sps made, remove marker, work ch1, skip a st, (1dc, ch1, 1dc, ch1, 1dc) in corner st, replace marker in the center dc of the corner group just made. Continue to work ch-1 sps on the remaining sides, working the corner groups in the marked sts and placing the marker in the center dc. End with a sl st to the 3rd of ch-4.

Note: There are 28 x ch-1 sps between the marked corner dcs.

Round 10   ch1, 1sc beside ch-1, *ch3, skip (1ch, 1dc, 1ch), work (1dc, 1 x ch4 picot, ch1, 1dc) in next dc, ch3, skip (1ch, 1dc, 1ch), 1sc (tight) in next dc, repeat from* 2 more times, ch3, skip (1ch, 1dc, 1ch). Remove the marker, work a double picot group in the corner dc as follows: (1dc, 1 x ch4 picot, ch1, 1dc, 1 x ch4 picot, ch1, 1dc). **ch3, skip (1ch, 1dc, 1ch), 1sc in next dc, ch3, skip (1ch, 1dc, 1ch), work (1dc, 1 x ch4 picot, ch1, 1dc) in next dc, repeat from** along the remaining sides, working a double picot group in the corners as before. End with a sl st to sc at the beginning of the round. Finish off, weave in ends.

TO COMPLETE. Press lightly on the wrong side, using a steam iron and a damp cloth. Ease into shape. If necessary, pin out, while still damp. Allow to dry. The first motif is now finished. Read the next paragraph carefully before completing the 2nd motif.

LINKING THE MOTIFS
Refer to diagram 2, on page 92, for the linking order. With right side facing, start on the second motif. After completing round 9, proceed with round 10, but leave 1 complete side and the final half row unfinished, ending with the center corner dc of the double picot group. Hold the loop with a safety pin and press the unfinished motif lightly on the wrong side before linking it. *Work ch2 of the next ch4 picot, insert the hook in the picot on the opposite motif (inserting the hook in the wrong side/back of the picot), sl st to link. Work the remaining ch2 of the picot and a sl st to the first of ch4, ch1, 1dc in same st as last dc, ch3, skip (1ch, 1dc, 1ch), 1sc in next dc, ch3, skip (1ch, 1dc,1ch), 1dc in next dc, repeat from*, linking the motifs together till 8 picots have been crocheted

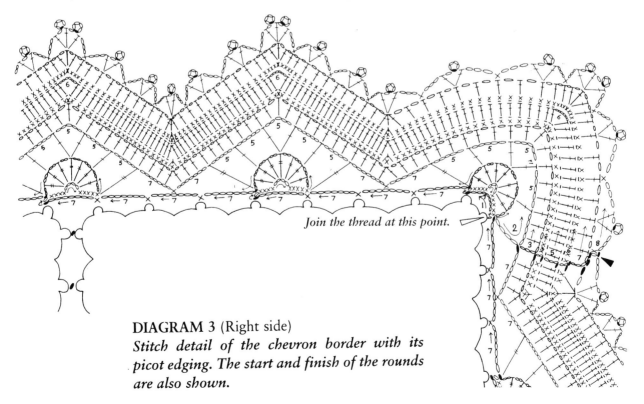

Join the thread at this point.

DIAGRAM 3 (Right side)
Stitch detail of the chevron border with its picot edging. The start and finish of the rounds are also shown.

together. Continue to complete the corner group and the last half row. End with a sl st to the sc at the beginning of the round. Finish off .

Continue adding motifs in this way until you have obtained the required length, then begin to add the second row of motifs. When a motif is to be linked along **2** of its sides to another, remember to leave **2** sides, and the last half row of the third, unworked. The chevron border will fit any size or shape, square or oblong.

CHEVRON BORDER WITH A PICOT EDGE

Note: Marking the stitches at this stage is even more important and will ensure a perfect finish.

Round 1 Right side facing. Join the thread by tying it to the right hand picot of the double picot group, as shown on diagram 3, page 93. Draw a working loop through as before, ch1, 1sc beside ch1. Work an open trc 'shell' as follows: ch7, sl st to the next picot, ch1, **turn**, (4sc, ch4, 4sc) in ch-7 loop, 1sc in next sc, **turn**, ch2, *1trc in ch-4 loop, ch2, repeat from* 6 more times, skip 4sc, sl st in the next st (8 x ch-2 sps made – or 1 open trc 'shell'). **ch-7, 1sc in the next picot, repeat from** till 3 x ch-7 loops made. Work 1 open trc 'shell' as before, repeat from** along the first full side, ending with 3 x ch-7 loops before the next corner. Work 1 open trc 'shell' over the next 2 corner picots. Now repeat the pattern sequence on the remaining 3 sides. End with a sl st to the sc at the beginning of the round. Do not turn.

Round 2 ch9 (to count as 1trc and ch-5), *skip (2ch, 1trc, 2ch), 1dc in next trc, ch5, skip (2ch, 1trc, 2ch), work (1dc, ch5, 1dc) in next trc, ch5, skip (2ch, 1trc, 2ch), 1dc in next trc, ch5, skip (ch2, 1trc, ch2), 1trc in next st, **ch7**, skip (7ch, 1sc, 3ch), 1sc (tight) in next ch st, **ch7**, skip (3ch, 1sc, 7ch), 1trc in sc at the beginning of the 'shell', ch5, repeat from* along the first full side, work around corner and continue to repeat the pattern sequence on the remaining 3 sides.

End the round by omitting the last trc and working a sl st to the 4th of ch-9 at the beginning of the round. Do not turn.

Note: Take extra care with this next round: mark each center dc at all points for future reference.

Round 3 ch4 (to count as 1dc and ch-1), skip st at base of ch-4, *1dc in next ch, ch1, skip 1ch, 1dc in next ch, ch1, skip 1ch, 1dc in next dc, 1ch, skip 1ch, repeat from* once more. Continue round the point as follows: 1dc in next ch, ch1, 1dc in **next** ch, **mark** the dc just made. ch1, 1dc in **next** ch, ch1, skip 1ch, 1dc in next dc. Continue to work ch-1 sps, skipping 1ch between sts till 10 x ch-1 sps are made from the marked dc, ch1, skip 1ch, decrease next 2dcs as follows: in next ch, work 1dc to the last stage but one (2 loops left on the hook), skip (1ch, 1sc, 1ch). In the next ch, work 1dc to the last stage but one (3 loops left on hook), yo and draw through all 3 loops (decrease complete). Continue to repeat the pattern sequence, increasing and decreasing as required on the remaining 3 sides. End with a sl st to the 3rd of ch-4 at the beginning of the round (23sps between marked dcs). Do not turn.

Note: Work all sts on rounds 4, 5 and 6 extra firmly.

Round 4 ch2, *1sc in sp, 1sc in dc, repeat from* till you reach the marked st, remove the marker, work 3sc in the next st, **mark** the center sc, *1sc in sp, 1sc in dc, repeat from* till 21sc are made, from the marked sc (10sps from corner point). Decrease scs over the next 3sts as follows: insert the hook in the next sp, draw the thread through, hook in the next st, draw the thread through, hook in the next sp, draw the thread through (4 loops now on hook), yo and draw through all 4 loops on the hook (3sc decrease complete).

Note: You may find it useful to mark under the top 2 threads of decrease for future reference. Continue st sequence, 1sc in dc, 1sc in sp, increasing and decreasing, replacing the markers as required. Refer to diagram 3. End with a sl st to ch-2. Do not turn.

Round 5 ch3, 1dc in each st, working into the **back single thread only**, till you reach the marked st at the point (see diagram), * remove the marker, work (1dc, ch6, 1dc) in that st, work 1dc in each st till 21sts are made, from ch-6 sp. Decrease the next 2dcs as follows: work 1dc in next st to the last stage but one (2 loops on hook), **skip** the marked st (decrease on the row before), work 1dc in the next st to the last stage but one (3 loops on hook), yo and draw through all 3 loops on the hook (2dc decrease is complete). Work 1dc in each next 20sts. Continue to repeat the pattern sequence from* on the remaining sides. End with 1dc in each of the remaining 3sts after the **last** 2dc decrease, sl st to 3rd of ch-3. Do not turn (22dcs between decrease and increase markers). Check your work frequently to keep the stitch count accurate and adjust if necessary.

Round 6 ch2, 1sc in each st, working into the **back single thread only**, till you reach the corner sp (17sc), *7sc in ch-6 loop, **mark the center sc** of 7sc, 1sc in each st till 23 sc from the marked corner sc, decrease the next 3sc, 1sc in each next 20sts till you reach the corner sp. Continue to repeat the pattern sequence from* on the remaining sides. End with 1sc in each remaining 2sts after **last** 3sc decrease, sl st to the second of ch-2, **sl st again** in next sc. Do not turn.

Round 7 ch4, skip st at the base of ch-4 and next st, 1dc in next st, (under **2** threads), *ch1, skip a st, 1dc in next st, repeat from* till 9sps made, ch1, skip a st, remove marker, work (1dc, ch1, 1dc, ch1, 1dc) in stitch at point, replace the marker in the center dc of the corner group. **ch1, skip a st, 1dc in next st, repeat from** till 11 sps from marked st are made, ch1, skip a st, decrease next 3dc as follows: work 1dc in next st to the last stage but one, **skip** 1sc, 1dc in next st to the last stage but one, **skip** 1sc, 1dc in the next st to the last stage but one, yo and draw through all 4 loops on hook, **mark** this decrease for future reference. Continue to repeat the pattern sequence, checking the diagram to ensure the correct placing of the increases / decreases and of the space count between the marked sts. The space count from here will be 12 x ch-1 sps between increase and decrease markers. Complete all sides, including the last 3dc decrease on the last side. End with ch1, a sl st to the 3rd of ch-3, a sl st **again** in the next ch and the next dc. ch1. Do not turn.

Round 8 1sc beside ch1, *ch3, skip (1ch, 1dc, 1ch), work (1dc, 1 x ch4 picot, ch1, 1dc) in the next dc, ch3, skip (1ch, 1dc, 1ch), 1sc (tightly) in the next dc, repeat from* once more. ch3, skip (1ch, 1dc 1ch), remove the marker, work a double picot group in the corner dc as follows: (1dc, 1 x ch4 picot, ch1, 1dc, 1 x ch4 picot, ch1, 1dc). Continue to repeat the pattern sequence on the remaining sides till the last single picot group is complete. End with ch3, skip 1ch, sl st to sc at the beginning of the round. Finish off, weave in tail ends.

TO COMPLETE
Press lightly on the wrong side, using a damp cloth. Ease gently into shape on a flat surface, covered in plastic wrap. Allow to dry.

SCOTTISH THISTLE DOILY

Approximate size: 16 in square

MATERIALS. 3½ oz / 90 g white bedspread-weight cotton thread No 10, a No 7 / 1.50 mm crochet hook

STITCHES, ABBREVIATIONS & SYMBOLS

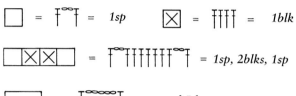

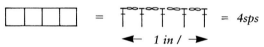

TENSION / GAUGE

WORKING NOTES

- ch2 between dcs on open mesh
- Work in same direction on each round, following the stitch diagrams as you work.
- Keep the tension firm and even throughout.
- ch3 at the start of a round count as 1dc.
- ch5 at the start of a round count as 1dc and ch2.

BEGIN. (See diagram 1 on page 98), ch9, sl st to form a ring.

Round 1 ch5, 1dc in ring, *ch5, 1dc in ring, ch2, 1dc in ring, repeat from* 2 more times, ch5, sl st to the 3rd of ch-5. Do not turn.

Round 2 ch3, 2dc in ch-2 sp, 1dc in dc, ch2,

(1dc, ch5, 1dc) in the center ch of ch-5, ch2, skip 2ch, 1dc in dc, 2dc in ch-2 sp, 1dc in dc, ch2, skip 2ch, repeat from 2 more times. End with (1dc, ch5, 1dc) in the center ch of ch-5, ch2, skip 2ch, sl st to the 3rd of ch-3.

Round 3 ch3, 1dc in each next 3dc, *ch3, skip 2ch, 1sc (tightly) in next dc, ch3, skip 2ch, (1dc, ch5, 1dc) in the center ch of ch-5, ch3, skip 2ch, 1sc in next dc, ch3, skip 2ch, 1dc in each next 4dc, repeat from* 2 more times. End with ch3, skip 2ch, 1sc in next dc, ch3, skip 2ch, (1dc, ch5, 1dc) in the center ch of ch-5, ch3, skip 2ch, 1sc (tightly) in next dc, ch3, sl st to the 3rd of ch-3.

Round 4 to round 33 Follow diagram 2 on page 98, working blocks and spaces. **Remember the rule:** if there is a **block** at the beginning of the round, work ch3, 2dc in sp or in **dcs**, 1dc in next dc. If there is a **space** at the beginning of the round, work ch5, skip **2ch** or **2dc**, 1dc in next dc. End round 33 with a sl st to the 3rd of ch-5.

Note: Every few rounds, check to make sure that the work lies flat. If **not,** re-work from where the 'waving' begins, and try to keep the tension consistent throughout.

FINAL EDGE. Follow diagram 3 on page 99 for stitch detail.

Round 34 ch3, 2dc in sp, 1dc in next dc, *ch3, skip 2ch, 1sc in next dc, ch3, skip 2ch, 1dc in dc, 2dc in sp, 1dc in next dc, repeat from* till 11 x 4dc blks are complete, ch3, skip 2ch, 1sc in next dc, ch3, skip 2ch, 1dc in next dc, (3dc,

DIAGRAM 1
(Right side)

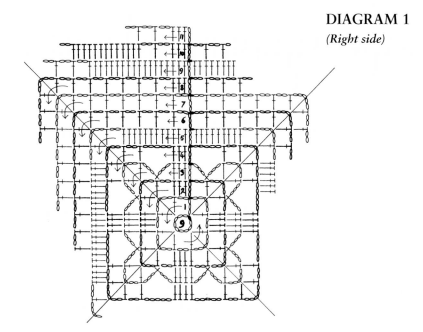

DIAGRAM 2

(Right side)

Center

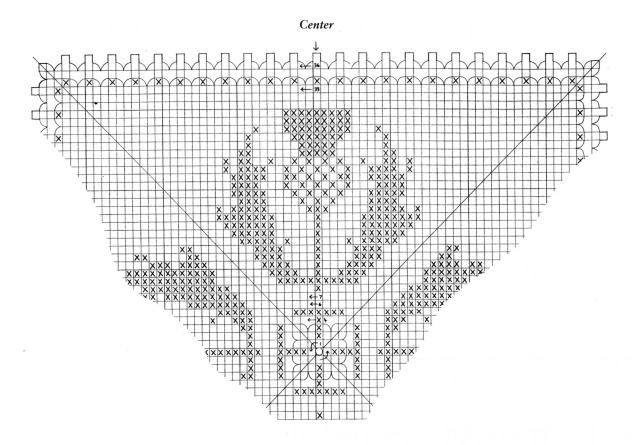

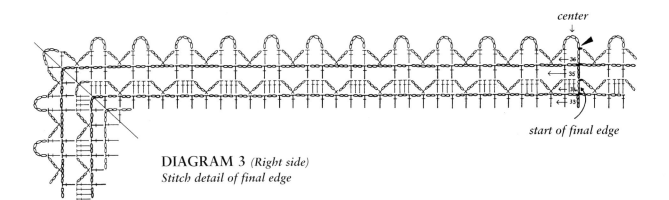

center

36
35
34
33

start of final edge

DIAGRAM 3 *(Right side)*
Stitch detail of final edge

ch5, 3dc) in ch-5 corner loop, 1dc in next dc. Continue to work the remaining sides and the corners as before, following the diagram. End with a sl st to the 3rd of ch-3 at the beginning of the round.

Round 35 ch5, skip 2dc, 1dc in next dc, *ch5, skip (3ch, 1sc, 3ch), 1dc in dc, ch2, skip 2dc, 1dc in dc, repeat from* till you reach the corner sp. Work ch2, (1dc, ch5, 1dc) in the center ch of ch-5, ch2, 1dc in dc, ch2, skip 2dc, 1dc in dc. Continue to work the remaining sides and corners as before. End with ch5, sl st to the 3rd of ch-5 at the beginning of the round.

Round 36 ch9, to count as 1dc and ch-6, skip 2ch, 1dc in next dc, *ch3, skip 2ch, 1sc (tightly) in next ch, ch3, skip 2ch, 1dc in next dc, ch6,

skip 2ch, 1dc in next dc, repeat from* till 12 x ch-6 loops have been made, ch3, skip 2ch, 1sc in next dc, ch3, (1dc, ch6, 1dc) in the center ch of ch-5, ch3, skip 2ch, 1dc in next dc. Continue to work the remaining sides and corners as before, till you have worked the last ch-6 loop and 1dc in dc. End with ch3, skip 2ch, 1sc in next ch, ch3, skip 2ch, sl st to the 3rd of ch-9 at the beginning of the round. Finish off, weave in ends.

TO COMPLETE. Press lightly on the wrong side, using a damp cloth. To make sure that the doily is absolutely square, draw a square on a piece of paper. Place it on a board and cover it with plastic wrap. Finally, pin the doily on to the board, using the drawn shape to guide you. Allow to dry fully.

Overleaf. The Scottish thistle doily

FILIGREE LACE DOILY

Approximate size: 11 in x 9 in

MATERIALS. 1 oz / 20 g pale yellow or white bedspread weight cotton No 10 – a No 7 / 1.50 mm crochet hook

SPECIAL STITCHES

= *ch5 bar*

= *lacet*

WORKING NOTES

◆ Written instructions are given for the first few rounds to familiarize you with the 'bar and lacet' technique. The complete pattern is shown in the diagram on page 102.

◆ Photocopy this diagram, coloring in each round lightly as you work.

◆ The increases appear in bold (darker lines) on the diagram.

◆ Work in the same direction throughout (right side facing). All chains and stitches must be firm and even.

◆ Mark the 3rd ch of the starting chain as you begin each round as a guide to the correct placing of the sl st at the **end** of each round. Remove and replace the markers as required.

BEGIN. ch29.

Round 1   1dc in 8th ch from hook, *ch2, skip 2ch, 1dc in next ch, repeat from* till 7 x ch-2 spaces made, ch2, skip 2ch, (1dc, ch2) 5 times in the last ch. This will have turned your work(still with right side facing) ready to work along the underside of the foundation chain. Continue: skip 2ch, *1dc in next ch, ch2, skip 2ch, repeat from* 6 more times, (1dc, ch2) 4 times in next ch. End by skipping 1ch, sl st to next ch at the beginning of the round (see diagram).

Round 2   ch6 (to count as 1dc and ch-3), skip 2ch, 1sc in next dc, ch3, skip 2ch, 1dc in next dc (the first lacet is made), work the next lacet as follows: *(ch3, skip 2ch, 1sc in next dc, ch3, skip 2ch, 1dc in next dc), repeat from* till 5 lacets are made, work ch3, 1dc in the same dc as last dc, repeat from* again, along other side till another 6 lacets are made, ch3, 1dc in the same dc as the last dc, ch3, skip 2ch, 1sc in next dc, ch3, skip 2ch. End with a sl st into 3rd of ch-6 at the beginning of the round.

Round 3   ch8 (to count as 1dc and 1 x ch5 bar), skip (3ch, 1sc, 3ch), 1dc in next dc, *ch5, skip (3ch, 1sc, 3ch), 1dc in next dc (2nd ch5 bar is made), repeat from* till 4 bars are made, ch3, 1dc in same dc as last dc, ch5, skip (3ch, 1sc, 3ch), work (1dc, ch3, 1dc) in next dc, ch3, skip 3ch, (1dc, ch3, 1dc) in next dc, ch5, skip (3ch, 1sc, 3ch), work (1dc, ch3, 1dc) in next dc, **ch5, skip (3ch, 1sc, 3ch), 1dc in next dc, repeat from** 3 more times, ch3, 1dc in same 3ch), work (1dc, ch3, 1dc) in next dc, ch3, skip 3ch, (1dc, ch3, 1dc) in next dc, ch5, skip (3ch, 1sc, 3ch), 1dc at the base of ch-8. End with ch3, sl st to the 3rd of ch-8.

Note: (1dc, ch3, 1dc) worked in the same stitch is an increase (8 increases on round 3).

Round 4 ch6 (to count as 1dc and ch-3), skip 2ch, 1sc in next ch, ch3, skip 2ch, 1dc in next dc (lacet made), *ch3, skip 2ch, 1sc in next ch, ch3, skip 2ch, 1dc in next dc, repeat from* 2 more times, ch5, skip 3ch, 1dc in next dc, ch3, skip 2ch, 1sc in next ch, ch3, skip 2ch, 1dc in next dc, ch5, skip 3ch, 1dc in next dc, ch3, skip 3ch, 1dc in next dc, ch5, skip 3ch, 1dc in next dc, ch3, skip 2ch, 1sc in next ch, ch3, skip 2ch, 1dc in next dc, ch5, skip 3ch, 1dc in next dc, *ch3, skip 2ch, 1sc in next ch, ch3, skip 2ch, 1dc in next dc, repeat from* 3 more times, ch5, skip 3ch, 1dc in next dc, ch3, skip 2ch, 1sc in next ch, ch3, skip 2ch, 1dc in next dc, ch5, skip 3ch, 1dc in next dc, ch3, skip 3ch, 1dc in next dc, ch5, skip 3ch, 1dc in next dc, ch3, skip 2ch, 1sc in next ch, ch3, skip 2ch, 1dc in next dc. End with ch5, skip 3ch, sl st to 3rd of ch-6. You may find it useful to tie a contrasting thread around the ch-3 at each end of the oval on round 4 (see diagram). These markers can be left in till the doily is complete

Filigree doily – right side

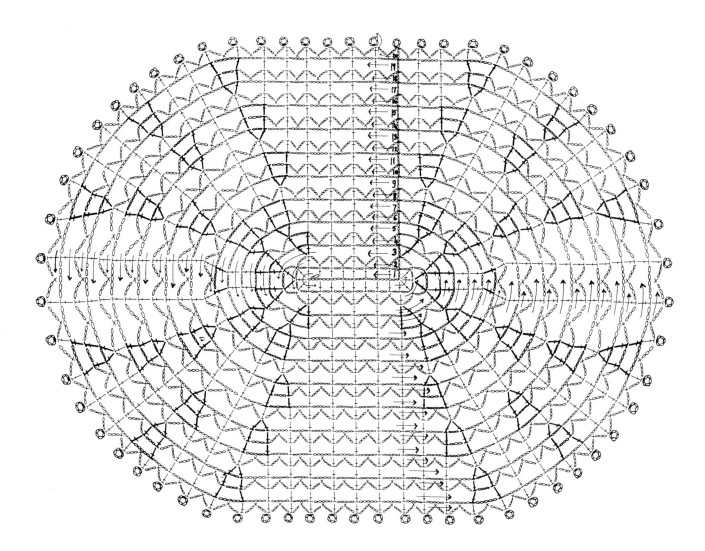

Round 5 to round 20 Continue, following the stitch diagram. Take extra care at all stages: the correct placing of the increases, marked in bold on the diagram, is vital. As each round becomes bigger, the stitch arrangement around each end of the oval shape changes slightly.

Detail for round 20: ch8, sl st to 5th ch from hook (making 1 x ch5 picot), ch3, skip 2ch, 1sc in next ch, ch3, skip 2ch, *(1dc, 1 x ch5 picot) in next dc, ch3, skip 2ch, 1sc in next ch, ch3, skip 2ch, repeat from* till round. End with a sl st to the 3rd of ch-8 at the beginning of the round. Finish off, weave in end

TO COMPLETE
Press lightly on the wrong side, using a damp cloth. Ease gently into shape, over a board covered in plastic wrap, pinning out the picots evenly all round.

Below. The filigree doily worked in white. Overleaf. The yellow version of the filigree doily.

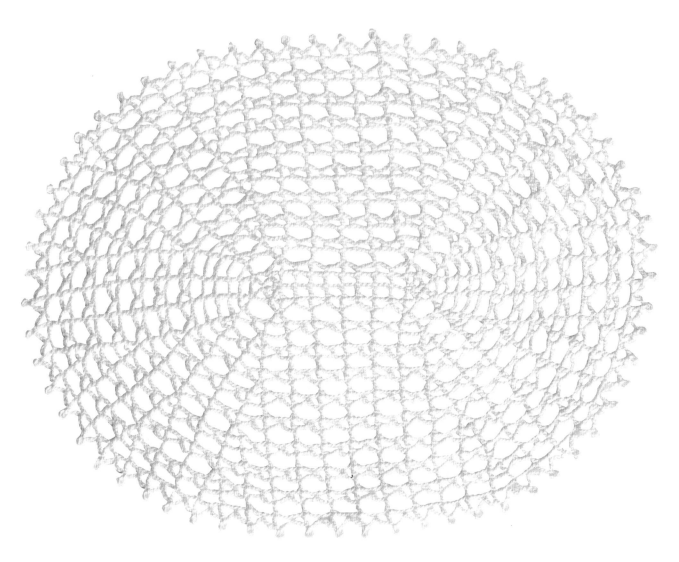

AUTUMN LEAVES DOILY

Approximate size: 8½ in in diameter

MATERIALS. 1 oz / 20 g écru or white bedspread-weight cotton thread / No 10, a No 7 / 1.50 mm crochet hook

WORKING NOTES

- ch3 at the beginning of the round count as 1dc.
- Make a photocopy of the diagram on page 106 and color each round as you work.
- Work in the same direction on each round and tighten all chs, scs and dcs as you finish each stitch.

BEGIN. ch10, sl st to form a ring.

Round 1 ch3 (to count as 1dc), 23dc in the ring, (24dc including ch3), sl st to the 3rd of ch-3, do not turn.

Round 2 ch1, 1sc beside ch1, ch5, *skip 2dc, 1sc in next dc, ch5, repeat from* till round. End with a sl st in the first sc at the beginning of the round (8 x ch-5 loops made). Sl st in each next 3ch of the first ch-5 loop.

Round 3 ch8, *1sc in the next ch-5 loop, ch8, repeat from* till round. End with a sl st to the first ch of ch-8, sl st **again** in next ch.

Round 4 ch3, 10dc in first loop, 11dc in each next 7 loops. End with a sl st to the 3rd of ch-3 at the beginning of the round (8 x 11dc groups made).

Note: from now on, mark the start of each round.

Round 5 ch6 (to count as 1dc and ch-3), 1dc in the space directly below ch-6, ch5, 1sc (tightly) in the center dc of the 11dc group, ch5, skip 5dc, *(1dc, ch3, 1dc) in the space between the next two 11dc groups, ch5, skip 5dc, 1sc (tightly) in next dc, ch5, skip 5dc, repeat from* till round. End with a sl st to the 3rd of ch-6.

Round 6 ch3, 4dc in ch-3 space, ch3, 1sc in ch-5 loop, ch3, 1sc in next ch-5 loop, ch3, *5dc in ch-3 space, ch3, 1sc in ch-5 loop, ch3, 1sc in next ch-5 loop, ch3, repeat from* till round. End with a sl st to the 3rd of ch-3.

Round 7 ch3, 1dc in the st at the base of ch-3, 1dc in each next 3dc, 2dc in next dc, ch5, skip 3ch, 1sc in next ch-3 loop, ch5, skip next 3ch, *2dc in next dc, 1dc in each next 3dc, 2dc in next dc, ch5, skip 3ch, 1sc in next ch-3 loop, ch5, skip 3ch, repeat from* till round. End with a sl st to the 3rd of ch-3.

Round 8 ch3, 1dc in st at the base of ch-3, 1dc in each next 5dc, 2dc in next dc, ch3, 1sc in ch-5 loop, ch3, 1sc in next ch-5 loop, ch3, *2dc in next dc, 1dc in each next 5dc, 2dc in next dc, ch3, 1sc in the ch-5 loop, ch3, 1sc in the next ch-5 loop, ch3, repeat from* till round. End with a sl st to the 3rd of ch-3.

Round 9 ch3, 1dc in each next 6dc, decrease

last 2dc, ch7, skip 3ch, 1sc in next ch-3 loop, ch7, skip 3ch, *decrease next 2dc, 1dc in each next **5dc**, decrease next 2dc, ch7, skip 3ch, 1sc in next ch-3 loop, ch7, skip 3ch, repeat from* till round. End with a sl st in the first dc at the beginning of the round, **not** the ch-3.

Round 10   ch3, 1dc in each next 4dc, decrease next 2dc, ch5, 1sc in ch-7 loop, ch5, 1sc in next ch-7 loop, ch5, *decrease next 2dc, 1dc in each next **3dc**, decrease next 2dc, ch5, 1sc in ch-7 loop, ch5, 1sc in next ch-7 loop, ch5, repeat from* till round. End with a sl st in the first dc, **not** the ch-3.

Round 11   ch3, 1dc in each next 2dc, decrease next 2dc, ch5, 1sc in ch-5 loop, ch5, 5dc in next ch-5 loop, ch5, 1sc in next ch-5 loop, ch5, decrease next 2dc, **1dc** in next dc, decrease next 2dc, ch5, 1sc in ch-5 loop, ch5, continue the stitch sequence as shown on diagram till round. End with a sl st to the first dc, **not** the ch-3.

Round 12   ch3, decrease next 2dc, ch3, 1sc in ch-5 loop, ch3, 1sc in the next ch-5 loop, ch3, 2dc in first dc, 1dc in each next 3dc, 2dc in next dc, ch3, 1sc in ch-5 loop, ch3, 1sc in next ch-5 loop, ch3, decrease next 3dc, ch3, 1sc in ch-5 loop, ch3, 1sc in next ch-5 loop, ch3, continue the stitch sequence as shown on the diagram till round. End with a sl st to the first dc, **not** the ch-3.

Round 13   ch8 (to count as 1dc and ch-5), skip

Doily (right side)

3ch, 1sc in next loop, ch5, skip 3ch, 2dc in first dc, 1dc in each next 5dc, 2dc in next dc, ch5, skip 3ch, 1sc in next ch-3 loop, ch5, skip 3ch, 1dc in st on top of 3dc decrease, ch5, skip 3ch, 1sc in next ch-3 loop, ch5, continue the stitch sequence as shown on the diagram till the end of the round. End with a sl st to the 3rd of ch-8.

Round 14   ch6 (to count as 1dc and ch-3), 1dc in st at base of ch-6, ch5, skip 5ch, 1sc in next ch-5 loop, ch5, decrease next 2dc, 1dc in each next 5dc, decrease next 2dc, ch5, 1sc in ch-5 loop, ch5, skip 5ch, (1dc, ch3, 1dc) in dc, ch5, skip 5ch, 1sc in next ch-5 loop, ch5, continue the stitch sequence as shown on diagram till the end of the round. End with a sl st to the 3rd of ch-6.

Round 15   ch3, 1dc in st at base of ch-3, ch5, skip 3ch, 2dc in next dc, ch5, skip 5ch, 1sc in next ch-5 loop, ch5, decrease next 2dc, 1dc in each next 3dc, decrease next 2dc, ch5, 1sc in ch-5 loop, ch5, skip 5ch, 2dc in next dc, ch5, skip 3ch, 2dc in next dc, ch5, skip 5ch, 1sc in next ch-5 loop, ch5, continue the stitch sequence as shown on diagram till the end of the round. End with a sl st to the 3rd of ch-3.

Round 16   ch3, 1dc in next dc, ch3, skip 2ch, 2dc in next **ch st**, ch3, skip 2ch, 1dc in each next 2dc, ch5, skip 5ch, 1sc in next ch-5 loop, ch5, decrease next 2dc, 1dc in next dc, decrease next 2dc, ch5, 1sc in next ch-5 loop, ch5, skip 5ch, 1dc in each next 2dc, continue the stitch sequence as shown on diagram till the end of the round. End with a sl st to the 3rd of ch-3.

Round 17   ch3, 1dc in next dc, ch5, skip 3ch, 1dc in each next 2dc, ch5, skip 3ch, 1dc in each next 2dc, ch5, skip 5ch, 1sc in next ch-5 loop, ch5, decrease next 3dc, ch5, 1sc in next ch-5 loop, ch5, skip 5ch, 1dc in each next 2dc, continue the stitch sequence as shown on diagram till the end of the round. End with a sl st to the 3rd of ch-3.

Round 18   ch3, 1dc in next dc, **ch6**, skip 5ch, 1dc in each 2dc, **ch6**, skip 5ch, 1dc in each next 2dc, **ch5**, skip 5ch, 1sc in next ch-5 loop, **ch3**, 1dc in st on top of 3dc decrease, **ch3**, 1sc in next ch-5 loop, **ch5**, skip 5ch, 1dc in each next 2dc, **ch6**, skip 5ch, continue the stitch sequence as shown on diagram till the end of the round. End with a sl st to the 3rd of ch-3.

Round 19   ch7, sl st in 4th ch from hook (this counts as 1dc and 1 x ch4 picot), ch1, 1dc in next dc, ch3, 1sc in ch-6 loop, ch3, 1dc in next dc, 1 x ch4 picot, ch1, 1dc in next dc, ch3, 1sc in ch-6 loop, ch3, 1dc in next dc, 1 x ch4 picot, ch1, 1dc in next dc, ch3, 1sc in ch-5 loop, ch3, skip 3ch, (1dc, 1 x ch4 picot, ch1, 1dc, 1 x ch4 picot, ch1, 1dc, 1 x ch4 picot, ch1, 1dc) in next dc, ch3, skip 3ch, 1sc in next ch-5 loop, ch3, continue the stitch sequence as shown on diagram till the end of the round. End with a sl st to the 3rd of ch-7 at the beginning of the round. Finish off, weave in ends.

TO COMPLETE. Press lightly on the wrong side, using a damp cloth. Ease gently into shape over a board covered in plastic wrap, pinning out the picots evenly all round.